INSTITUTE OF CZECH LITERATURE
KAROLINUM PRESS

CZECH LITERATURE STUDIES

PETR PLECHÁČ

Versification and Authorship Attribution

INSTITUTE OF CZECH LITERATURE
KAROLINUM PRESS

2021

INSTITUTE OF CZECH LITERATURE is a part of the Czech Academy of Sciences
Na Florenci 1420/3, 110 00 Prague 1, Czech Republic
www.ucl.cas.cz

KAROLINUM PRESS is a publishing department of Charles University
Ovocný trh 560/5, 116 36 Prague 1, Czech Republic
www.karolinum.cz

This study is the result of research funded by the Czech Science Foundation
as part of project GA ČR 17-01723S.

This publication was created with the support of Research Development Program RVO 68378068
and published with support from the Czech Academy of Sciences.

Language review by Debra Shulkes; technical language review by Benjamin Nagy
Cover and graphic design DesignIQ
Set and printed in the Czech Republic by Karolinum Press
First edition

Original manuscript reviewed by Mike Kestemont (University of Antwerp)
and Igor Pilshchikov (University of California, Los Angeles).

Cataloguing-in-Publication Data is available from the National Library of the Czech Republic.

ISBN 978-80-7658-027-5 (Institute of Czech Literature of the Czech Academy of Sciences)
ISBN 978-80-246-4871-2 (Karolinum Press)
ISBN 978-80-7658-028-2 (pdf, Institute of Czech Literature of the Czech Academy of Sciences)
ISBN 978-80-246-4890-3 (pdf, Karolinum Press)

https://doi.org/10.14712/9788024648903

Contents

Introduction

Contemporary stylometry is one of the fastest-growing fields in the computational study of literature. In recent years, a number of textual characteristics and machine learning techniques have proven highly accurate in distinguishing the texts of different authors. Many of these features like word and character *n*-gram frequencies amount, however, to what is known as statistical "rare events", or more precisely, a large number of rare events (LNRE). As a result, their analysis calls for fairly large text samples consisting of thousands or tens of thousands of words. Most theoretical studies in stylometry therefore focus on long novels. Poetry is usually omitted although we might expect to find many more cases of disputed authorship among poetic works.

At the same time, poetry has a number of specific versification features that are essentially Boolean or open to only a limited number of values. Some of these—stanza length and rhyme scheme, for example—are subject to the author's conscious selection and so unsuitable for authorship recognition. In contrast, others like the preference for certain rhythmic configurations or sound frequencies in rhyme may be outside the author's rational control. Although these characteristics have traditionally been recognised as author-specific (or at least period-specific), they have rarely featured in authorship attribution studies.

The goal of this book is to examine the applicability of these versification features to authorship attribution projects. To this end, I draw on poetic corpora in three different languages (Czech, German and Spanish) and apply this approach to two real-world cases of disputed authorship.

Chapter 1 gives a brief history of quantitative methods of authorship attribution with special attention to the methods used in this book.

Chapter 2 highlights different ways to capture versification features.

Chapter 3 describes experiments with versification-based attribution and compares the methods commonly used in stylometry.

Finally, Chapter 4 applies these findings to two actual cases of ambiguous authorship involving English- and Russian-language texts respectively. In the first case,

https://doi.org/10.14712/9788024648903.1

I attempt to determine which parts of the verse play *The Two Noble Kinsmen* were written by William Shakespeare and which were the work of his co-author, John Fletcher. In the second, working together with Artjoms Šeļa, I investigate the potential forgery of numerous 19th-century Russian poems that were originally attributed to Gavriil Stepanovich Batenkov. These poems first appeared in the 1978 edition of the poet's collected works, which was compiled by an established literary scholar—the main suspect in this intrigue.

Previous Publications

Chapter 1 expands on the opening sections of *Versification and authorship attribution. Pilot study on Czech, German, Spanish, and English poetry* (Plecháč, Bobenhausen and Hammerich 2018).

Czech versions of Chapters 1, 2 and 3 were submitted as part of my PhD thesis at Charles University in Prague, Czech Republic in 2019.

Data and Code

The data and code required to reproduce the analyses in this book can be found at ‹https://doi.org/10.5281/zenodo.4555250›.

HTML version

From early 2022, this book will also be available online at ‹https://versologie.cz/versification-authorship›.

1 Quantitative Approaches to Authorship Attribution

1.1 Origins of Stylometry

Many scholars (e.g. Holmes 1998; Juola 2006) trace the origins of stylometry to several passages in a letter written by the British mathematician Augustus De Morgan to Reverend W. Heald on August 18, 1851 (De Morgan 1851/1882). After considering how to distinguish the Pauline epistles actually written by St. Paul from those written by other author(s), De Morgan mused that the average word length measured by the number of characters might give some clue: "If St. Paul's epistles which begin with Παυλος gave 5.428 and the Hebrews gave 5.516, for instance, I should feel quite sure that the *Greek* of the Hebrews (passing no verdict on whether Paul wrote in Hebrew and another translated) was not from the pen of Paul" (De Morgan 1851/1882: 216; emphasis in the original). Later he complained: "If scholars knew the law of averages as well as mathematicians, it would be easy to raise a few hundred pounds to try this experiment on a grand scale" (De Morgan 1851/1882: 216).

In fact, it was not until the end of the 19th century that the American physicist Thomas Corwin Mendenhall raised the money for this experiment. In an initial article entitled "The Characteristic Curve of Composition" (1887), Mendenhall suggested ignoring averages and dealing with overall word length distribution instead. Eventually, thanks to the support of a benefactor, August Hemenway, he applied this method to a real-world case of disputed authorship. The results of that experiment were published in the article "A Mechanical Solution to a Literary Problem" (1901). There, Mendenhall compared the shape of a curve determined by the relative frequencies of words of different lengths in works ascribed to William Shakespeare with equivalent curves for works by Francis Bacon and Christopher Marlowe (FIG. 1.1). Based on the similarities and differences, he cautiously concluded that while Bacon had not written the works in question, there was strong evidence that Marlowe had (Mendenhall 1901: 104–105). The discrepancies between the curves for Shakespeare and Bacon were, however, later found to be due to the comparison of verse texts by the former with non-verse texts by the latter (see Williams 1975).

https://doi.org/10.14712/9788024648903.2

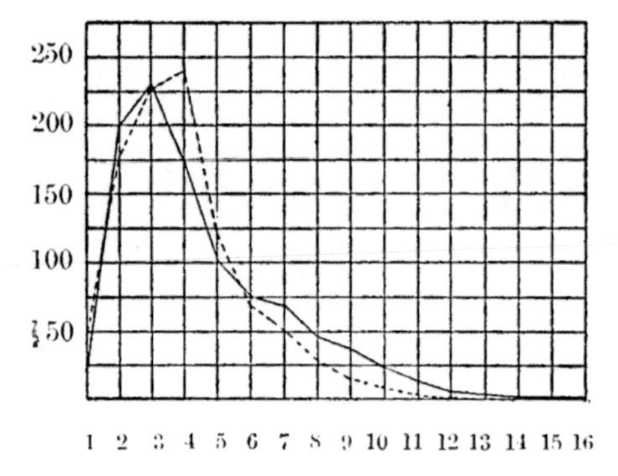

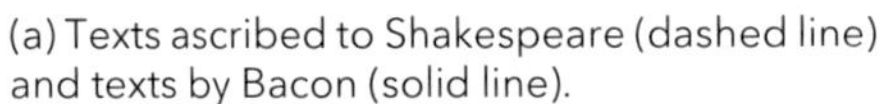

(a) Texts ascribed to Shakespeare (dashed line) and texts by Bacon (solid line).

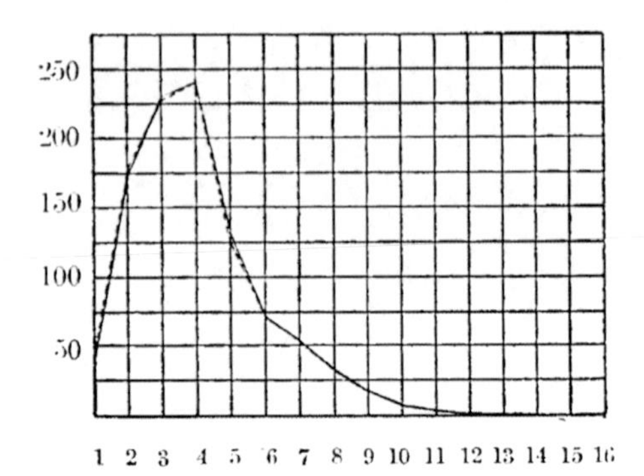

(b) Texts ascribed to Shakespeare (dashed line) and texts by Marlowe (solid line almost covering dashed line).

FIG. 1.1: Relative frequencies (per thousand) of word lengths measured by number of characters; source: Mendenhall 1901: 104 (facsimile).

Independently of Mendenhall, the American mathematician William Benjamin Smith had also been employing quantitative methods in the 1880s. In his article "Curves of Pauline and Pseudo-Pauline Style", published under the pen name Conrad Mascol (1888a; 1888b), he, like De Morgan, considered the authorship of the Pauline epistles. In line with Mendenhall, he took the shape of the curves representing various textual features (e.g. the average number of words or prepositions per page) to be a criterion. On comparing the curves for epistles generally agreed to be written by St. Paul with those of doubtful authorship, Smith concluded that the author of the former had probably not written the latter. Significantly, he also stressed that the key consideration when selecting features should be their topic independence.[1] This principle, though now taken for granted, was not generally accepted until the mid-20th century, as we will see in Section 1.2.

A third pioneering work usually mentioned in this field is an article by Lucius Adelno Sherman (1888) that was probably also conceived independently of Mendenhall's studies.[2] It analysed the average sentence length measured by the number of

1 Smith wrote: "When we now ask, What are the elements of style to be considered? The answer must be: All such as are affected not at all, or apparently and comparatively very little, by the subject-matters of discourse" (Mascol 1888a: 456).

2 Grzybek (2014) notes, however, that Sherman may have been inspired by a response to Mendenhall's initial article that was published in an 1887 issue of *Science*. Its author observed: "There are other characteristics of writers equally susceptible of treatment by the statistical and graphical method, in

words in the work of novelists writing in English. Still Sherman did not highlight the possibility of using this metric for authorship recognition.

Outside of these studies, there is, however, another branch of stylometry which, although only sporadically recognised by scholars (Grzybek 2014 and Grieve 2005 rank among the exceptions), dates back some 100 years before Mendenhall's first article and more than 60 years before De Morgan's letter. This concerns the attributions of Shakespearean scholars based on the quantification of rhythm and rhyme.

One of the earliest examples of this approach can be found in a study by Edmond Malone (1787/1803) which proposed that none of the three parts of the play *Henry VI* had actually been written by Shakespeare. Malone's arguments were based, among other things, on attention to versification: he argued that there were far fewer rhymes and enjambments in the texts in question than in other works by Shakespeare.

Another instance can be seen in a comment by the scholar Henry Weber about the play *The Two Noble Kinsmen* (1812), which was first published in 1634 as a collaborative work by William Shakespeare and John Fletcher (see Section 4.1 for details). Weber worked out a scene-by-scene division of authorship between Shakespeare and Fletcher based on the frequencies of certain line endings among other factors:

> Taking an equal number of lines in the different parts which are attributed to Shakespeare and to Fletcher, the number of female, or double terminations in the former, is less than one to four; on the contrary, in the scenes attributed to Fletcher the number of double or triple terminations is nearly three times that of single ones. (Weber 1812: 166)

Decades later, James Spedding (1850) used the same metric to arrive at a theory of joint authorship by Shakespeare and Fletcher that he also applied to *Henry VIII*.

The real rise of versification-oriented stylometry did not come, however, until the 1870s and 1880s after the founding of the *New Shakspere Society*.[3] In the first volume of their *Transactions*, one Society member, John Kells Ingram (1874) suggested dividing unstressed blank verse endings into "light endings" and "weak endings"[4] and using

which their personal peculiarities differ more widely, and which are therefore more characteristic than the habitual selection and use of long or short words. For example: it seems to me that the length of the sentence is such a peculiarity" (Eddy 1887: 297).

3 Concerning its name, the Society's members maintained: "This spelling of our great Poet's name is taken from the only unquestionably genuine signatures of his that we possess, the three on his will, and the two on his Blackfriars conveyance and mortgage." (Furnivall 1874a: 6).

4 Ingram described these two forms as follows: "It is evident that amongst what have been called as a class weak endings, there are different degrees of weakness. [...] There are *two* such degrees, which require to be discriminated, because on the words, which belong to one of these groups the voice can

the ratio of instances of the two to support Spedding's attribution of *Henry VIII*. Ingram himself called this method the "weak-ending test". Other members proposed (or adopted) and applied several other such verse tests designed to distinguish Shakespeare's works from those of other authors based on the prevalence of particular features. These included the "rhyme test" (for rhymed lines), the "stopt-line test" (for enjambment), the "middle-syllable test" (for extra-metrical syllables at the end of the first half-line) and the "caesura test" (for word breaks after the sixth syllable in alexandrines).[5]

Many of these attributions by New Shakspere Society members were later proven wrong owing to the simplistic nature of their methods or errors in their source data (Grieve 2005: 6). Even so, they are an important part of the history of stylometry and should not be neglected.

1.2 Searching for the "Golden Feature"

The works of George Kingsley Zipf seem to have inspired a new era in the development of 20th-century stylometry (see Koppel, Schler and Argamon 2009: 4–5). The formulation of Zipf's law (1932), which states that all natural language texts follow the same rank-frequency word distribution, likely encouraged scholars to rethink the possibilities for authorship attribution. This meant finding a similar textual feature that would remain stable across the works of one author while differing in those of other authors.

Of great influence in this period were the stylometric works of George Udny Yule, who initially proposed using sentence length measured by the number of words (Yule 1939). Unlike Sherman (see Section 1.1), Yule considered not only average values but also other distribution characteristics. These included the median, the $Q_{0,25}$ and $Q_{0,75}$ quartiles, the interquartile range and also—since sentence length generally tends to follow a positively skewed log-normal distribution—the decile $Q_{0,9}$.

Just a couple of years later, Yule's book *The Statistical Study of Literary Vocabulary* (1944) introduced a new metric designed to capture vocabulary richness. He defined that measure as follows:

to a certain small extent dwell, whilst the others are so essentially *proclitic* in their character [...] that we are forced to run them, in pronunciation no less than in a sense, into the closest connection with the opening words of the succeeding line. The former may with convenience be called 'light endings', whilst to the latter may be appropriated the name (hitherto vaguely given to both groups jointly) of 'weak endings'" (Ingram 1874: 447; emphasis in original).

5 See Fleay 1874a, 1874b, 1874c, 1874d; Furnivall 1874b, 1874c.

$$K = \frac{10^4\left[\left(\sum_{m=1}^{m_{\max}} m^2 V_m\right) - N\right]}{N^2} \tag{1.1}$$

where N is the text length measured by the number of tokens and V_m is the number of word types with a frequency of m.

Importantly, Yule did not take into account the entire vocabulary when he applied his metric to real attribution tasks. Instead, he confined his analysis to nouns alone. He explained this choice as follows:

> My object in limiting myself to nouns for the investigation into the vocabularies of Thomas à Kempis and Gerson was in part simply the limitation of material and the exclusion of words of little or no significance as regards style, such as prepositions, pronouns, etc. Of the three principal parts of speech, nouns, adjectives and verbs, I thought nouns would probably be the most significant or characteristic. (Yule 1944: 21).

In fact, it was fairly common for mid-20th-century scholars to assume that high-frequency function words had no authorial signal and, thus, could not contribute to authorship recognition (see Grieve 2005: 32–34). This assumption was wrong, however, as we will see in Section 1.3.

Many other simple features were proposed for authorship attribution purposes in this period. They included average word length measured by the number of syllables (Fucks 1952) and the frequency of loan words (Herdan 1956). None of them, however, turned out to be sufficiently robust, and when they were applied to attribution tasks other than those they were designed for, they usually failed (see Hoover 2003; Grieve 2005).

1.3 Multivariate Analyses

The most important contribution to 20th-century stylometry came from a publication by Frederick Mosteller and David L. Wallace (1964). In a groundbreaking study of the authorship of *The Federalist Papers*, the two revived a principle introduced by W. B. Smith (see Section 1.1) that remains widely accepted today. This held that as far as possible, the features used for authorship recognition should be topic independent. Rejecting the content-based word tests that dominated studies by their contemporaries, these scholars, thus, turned their gaze to the most common function words and the frequencies of their variations (e.g. *while/whilst*). Crucially, their analysis was based not on the usual comparison of isolated values but rather on one of entire sets. This is where the turn from simple univariate methods to more sophisticated multidimensional analyses began. By the 1980s, it had led to the application of such statistical methods as multivariate variance analysis (Larsen, Rencher and Layton 1980) and principal component analysis (Burrows and Hassal 1988; Burrows 1989). Of all of these methods, however, the so-called Burrows' Delta would prove the most popular.

1.3.1 Burrows' Delta

The Delta was proposed by John F. Burrows (2002, 2003) as a simple measure of stylistic similarities between two texts. This metric was primarily designed to resolve cases where there was a text of unknown or doubtful authorship (target text: t_0) and a corpus of works produced by a finite set of candidate authors (candidate set: $T = \{t_1, t_2, t_3, \dots, t_m\}$). The goal was to find the candidate whose texts showed the greatest similarity to the target text, i.e. the one whose texts had the lowest Delta value.

Like Mosteller and Wallace's analysis, Burrows' Delta relied on a set of high-frequency words. The most straightforward approach to such data would have been to plot their frequencies in both the target and the candidate texts and then compare the resulting curves just as Mendenhall had (Section 1.1). Such visual assessments tend, however, to be vague and unreliable. Instead, Burrows suggested an alternative: the discrepancy between the texts could be expressed as the mean value of the differences between the frequencies of specific words. This method was set out as follows:

(1) From the entire body of work (i.e. $t_0 \cup T$), select the n most common words $w_1, w_2, w_3, \dots, w_n$.
(2) Each text $t_i \in \{t_0, t_1, t_2, \dots, t_m\}$ is represented as a vector $\mathbf{f}_i = (f(t_{i,1}), f(t_{i,2}), \dots, f(t_{i,n}))$, where $f(t_{i,j})$ denotes the relative frequency of w_j in t_i.
(3) Word frequency tends to decrease sharply after the uppermost entries (Zipf's law). The differences in the prevalence of the most common words will, thus, generally be much larger than those between, say, the 50th and 100th most common words in any given body of texts. To make each word a marker of equal weight, the frequencies of individual words are transformed into *z*-scores: $\mathbf{t}_i = (z(t_{i,1}), z(t_{i,2}), \dots, z(t_{i,n}))$.

$$z\left(t_{i,j}\right) = \frac{f\left(t_{i,j}\right) - \mu_j}{\sigma_j} \tag{1.2}$$

$$\mu_j = \frac{1}{m}\sum_{i=0}^{m} f\left(t_{i,j}\right) \tag{1.3}$$

$$\sigma_j = \sqrt{\frac{1}{m}\sum_{i=0}^{m}\left(f\left(t_{i,j}\right) - \mu_j\right)^2} \tag{1.4}$$

The *z*-score transforms the frequency distribution for each word across the corpus to give it a mean of 0 and a standard deviation of 1. (In very rough terms, this transformation contracts or extends the frequency ranges so that they are approximately the same for each word.)

(4) The stylistic dissimilarity (Δ) between texts t_a and t_b is finally calculated as the arithmetic mean of the absolute values of the differences between the *z*-scores for individual words:

$$\Delta\left(t_a, t_b\right) = \frac{\sum_{j=1}^{n}\left|z\left(t_{a,j}\right) - z\left(t_{b,j}\right)\right|}{n} \tag{1.5}$$

(5) The candidate whose text $t_a \in T$ yields the lowest value $\Delta(t_a, t_0)$ is considered the most likely author of the target text.

To illustrate this approach, we may consider a model situation where Walter Scott's *The Lady of the Lake* is the target text and the candidate set consists of *Marmion* by the same author and *Childe Harold's Pilgrimage* by George Gordon Byron. FIG. 1.2a shows the relative frequencies of the 20 most common words in these three poetic works. FIG. 1.2b presents the data transformed into *z*-scores. FIG. 1.2c gives the absolute values of the differences between the *z*-scores for works in the candidate set and works in the target text. The last two columns highlight the mean values (Δ).

Thanks to the simple, intuitive and fairly accurate nature of the Delta measure, it was embraced soon after it was presented and became a popular authorship attribution method. Several modifications have since been proposed (e.g. Hoover 2004a, 2004b). From a contemporary perspective, however, the most important advance was arguably Shlomo Argamon's interpretation of the Delta's key principle.

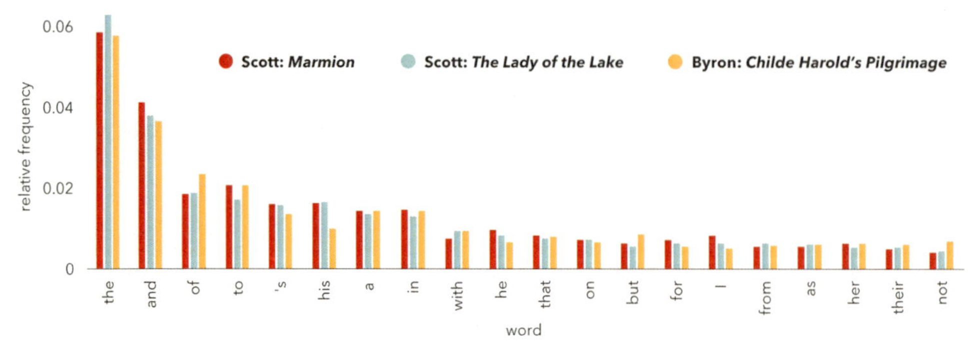

(a) Relative frequencies of the 20 most common words in each text.

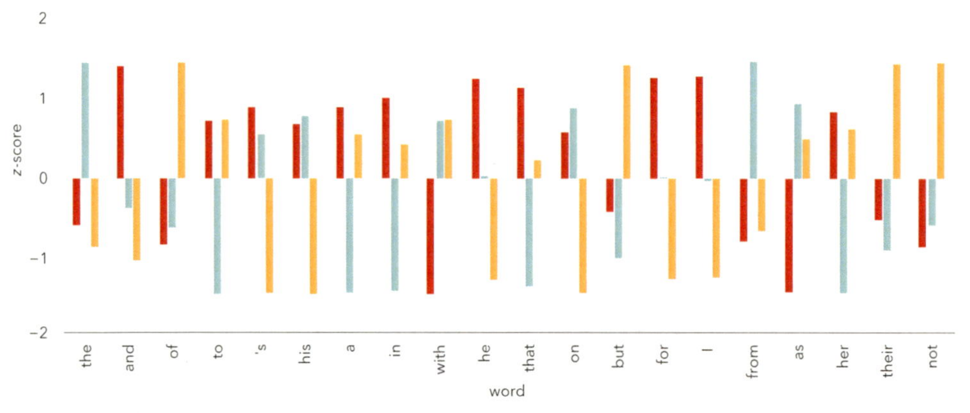

(b) Relative frequencies of the 20 most common words transformed into *z*-scores.

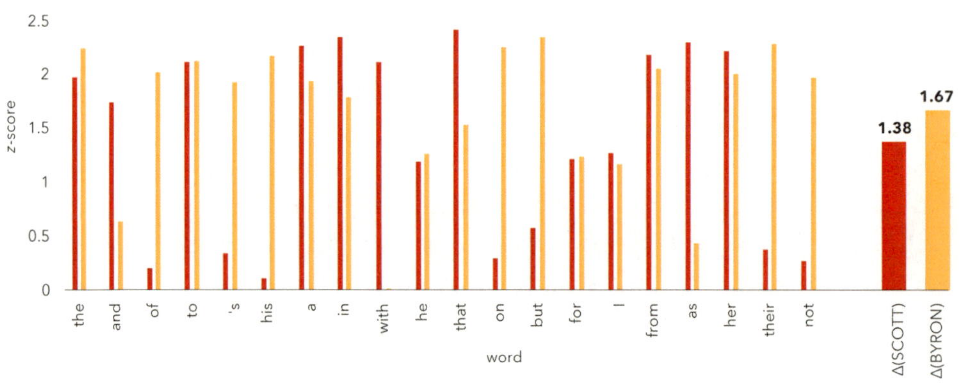

(c) Absolute values of the differences between the *z*-scores for each candidate and the target text; the final two columns show the mean values.

FIG. 1.2: Burrows' Delta for Walter Scott's *The Lady of the Lake* (target text), Walter Scott's *Marmion* and George Gordon Byron's *Childe Harold's Pilgrimage* (candidate set).

1.3.2 The Geometric Interpretation of Burrows' Delta and Its Modifications

Argamon (2008) pointed out that the Delta measure that Burrows had stumbled on by intuition was actually the equivalent of measuring the *Manhattan distance* between two vectors. As such, the entire method could be seen as an instance of nearest neighbour classification or a special case of the popular *k*-nearest neighbour classifier where $k = 1$.

Argamon proceeded from a simple consideration: Since the process was based on candidate ranking, there was no need to divide the sum of differences by the number of analysed words (n). After all, division by a constant would not affect the ranking. Once the denominator was dropped from formula 1.5, we obtain a simple summary of the absolute values of the *z*-score differences, i.e. the Manhattan distance (D_M; see FIG. 1.3):

$$\Delta(t_a, t_b) \propto D_M(\mathrm{t}_a, \mathrm{t}_b) = \sum_{j=1}^{n} \left| z(t_{a,j}) - z(t_{b,j}) \right| \tag{1.6}$$

In the same article, Argamon also suggested a modification of Burrows' original method, or what he called the quadratic Delta (Δ_Q) based on the Euclidean distance (D_E) between the given vectors:

$$D_E(\mathbf{t}_a, \mathbf{t}_b) = \sqrt{\sum_{i=1}^{n} \left(z(t_{a,i}) - z(t_{b,i}) \right)^2} \tag{1.7}$$

Just as dividing each distance by a constant did not affect the final ranking in Burrows' Delta, the same was true for extracting the root in the formula for the Euclidean distance (square root is a monotonically increasing function). The formula for Δ_Q was, thus, defined as the square of the Euclidean distance:

$$\Delta_Q(t_a, t_b) = \sum_{j=1}^{n} \left(z(t_{a,j}) - z(t_{b,j}) \right)^2 \tag{1.8}$$

The cosine Delta ($\Delta_\angle$; Smith and Aldridge 2011) is another recent popular modification of Burrows' Delta. It is based on the cosine similarity of vectors, that is, the cosine of the angle θ between them:

$$\cos(\theta) = \frac{\sum_{j=1}^{n} z(t_{a,j}) z(t_{b,j})}{\| \mathbf{t}_a \| \, \| \mathbf{t}_b \|} \tag{1.9}$$

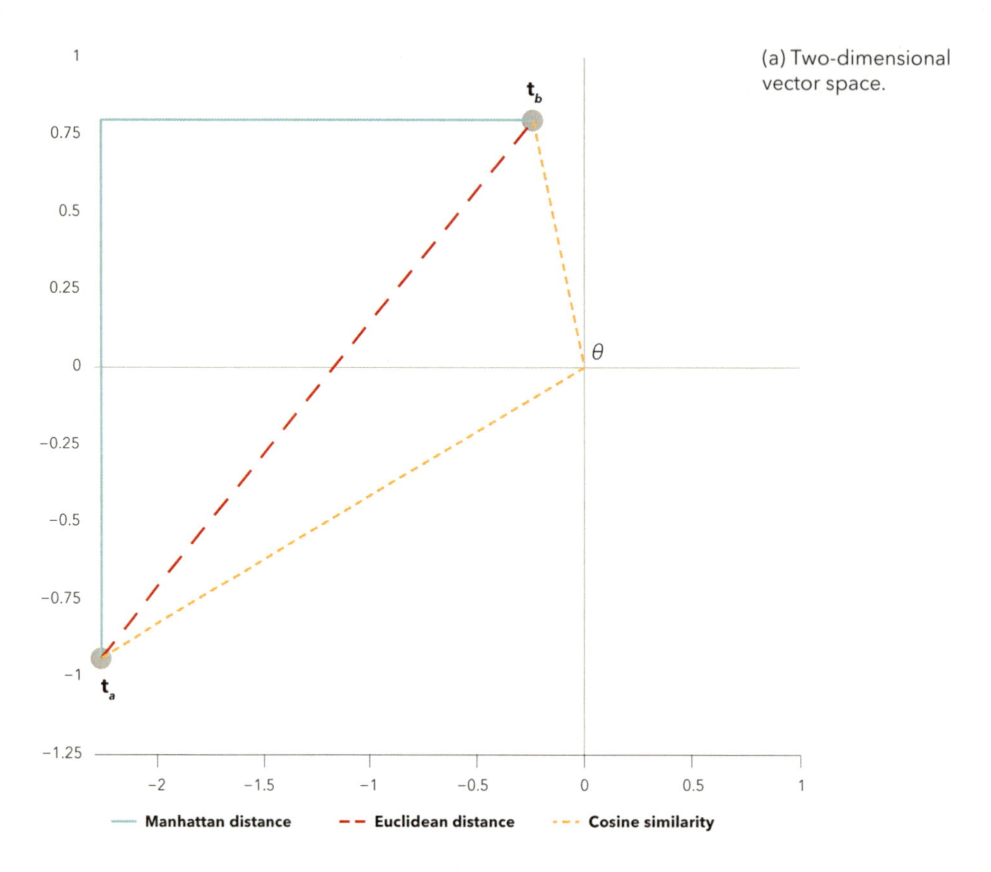

FIG. 1.3: Manhattan distance, Euclidean distance and cosine similarity of vectors $\mathbf{t}_a$ and $\mathbf{t}_b$.

Since $\cos(\theta) \in [-1, 1]$, the formula is modified so that—as with Burrows' Delta and the quadratic Delta—the greater the similarity between two texts, the lower the cosine Delta value and *vice versa*:

$$\Delta_{\angle}(t_a, t_b) = 1 - \cos(\theta) \tag{1.10}$$

Metrics from the Delta family have been tested across languages and text types with various settings for the number of the most common units (n) and with other features such as lemmata, character n-grams and word n-grams (see, e.g. Eder 2011; Rybicki and Eder 2011; Jannidis et al. 2015).

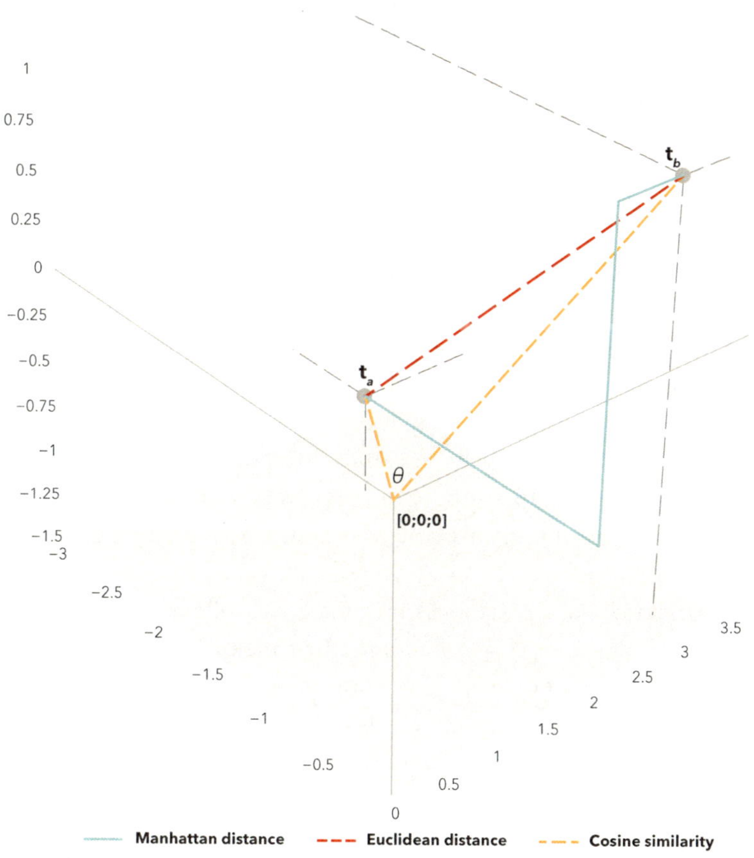

(b) Three-dimensional vector space.

1.4 Support-Vector Machines

Outside of the Delta, more sophisticated machine learning methods have gained increasing attention over the last decade or two. These include *random forest* (e.g. Tabata 2012), *naïve Bayes classifier* (e.g. Zhao and Zobel 2005) and above all *support-vector machine* (SVM) techniques (e.g. Diederich et al. 2003; Koppel and Schler 2004). The SVM technique is still probably the most popular in contemporary stylometry although deep-learning methods seem poised to overtake it (see, e.g. Savoy 2020). This section outlines the general principles behind SVM.

An SVM is a supervised learning technique, which means that its algorithm uses labelled training data to infer a classification function for new data. This key principle can be illustrated with a very simple example based on artificial data. Imagine a target text t_0 and 20 samples from each of two candidates (author 1, author 2). All of the texts are represented by z-scores for the two most common words ("the" and "and").

During the first (learning) phase, the SVM is fed data from author 1 and author 2 (training data). These data are labelled according to author, and the SVM tries to find a function that correctly separates them by their labels. This is done using a hyperplane—a subspace with one dimension fewer than the original vector space. In our example with its two-dimensional data, this means a one-dimensional space, i.e. a line. During the second phase (classification), the hyperplane inferred from the training data is used to classify the target text.

FIG. 1.4a shows that if the data are linearly separable, then an infinite number of potential hyperplanes can separate them correctly. Some of these may attribute the target text to author 1 while others may attribute it to author 2. From all these possibilities, the SVM chooses the hyperplane that maximises the distance to the nearest vectors on each side (also known as the support vectors), as shown in FIG. 1.4b (this is the maximum-margin hyperplane). In this case, the SVM classifies the target text as the work of author 1.

Generally, for n-dimensional data, the task is formulated as follows: We are given the training data $(\mathbf{x}_1, y_1), (\mathbf{x}_2, y_2), \ldots, (\mathbf{x}_m, y_m)$ where the first member of each pair denotes the n-dimensional vector $\mathbf{x}_i = (x_{i,1}, x_{i,2}, \ldots, x_{i,n})$ and the second member denotes one of two classes to which the vector belongs: $y_i \in \{-1, 1\}$. The goal is to find a normal vector $\mathbf{w}$ and a parameter b to define a hyperplane H

$$H : \mathbf{w} \cdot \mathbf{x} + b = 0 \tag{1.11}$$

that separates the vector space into two half-spaces so that each half-space contains only data of the same class and the distance to the nearest vector is maximised.

These requirements may be defined formally using the oriented distance d of the vectors $\mathbf{x}_i$ to hyperplane H. This will be positive for vectors in one half-space and negative for vectors in the other one:

$$d(\mathbf{x}_i, H) = \frac{\mathbf{x}_i \cdot \mathbf{w} + b}{\| \mathbf{w} \|} \tag{1.12}$$

As we have two classes $y_i \in \{-1, 1\}$, the requirement that each half-space contain vectors belonging to the same class may be formulated as:

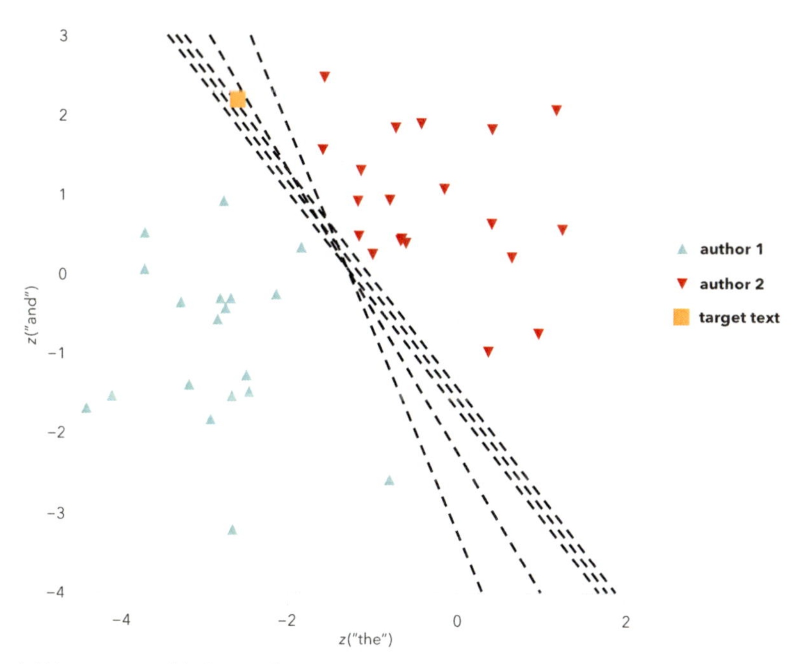

(a) Various possible hyperplanes separating training data from author 1 and author 2.

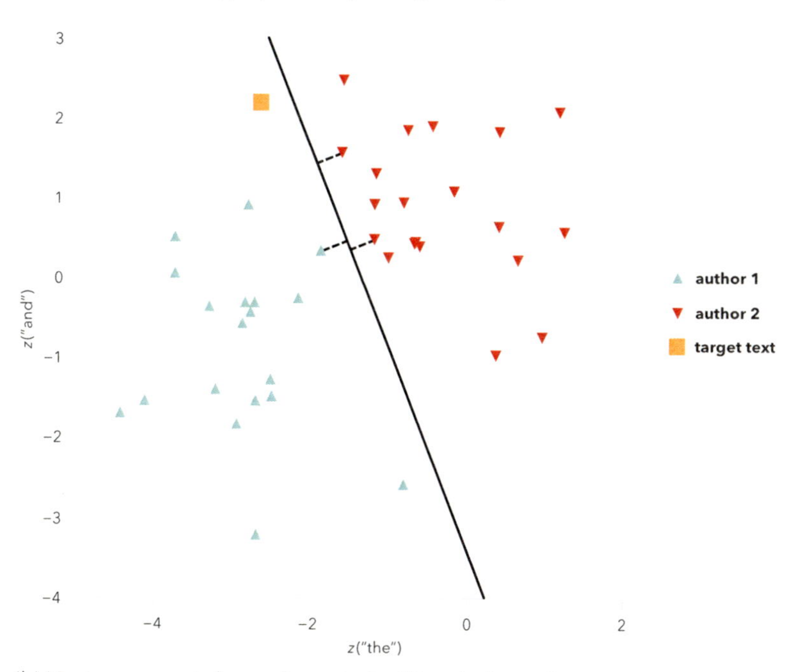

(b) Maximum-margin hyperplane; dashed lines indicate distances to support vectors.

FIG. 1.4: A Support-Vector Machine (artificial data).

$$\begin{aligned} \forall i : y_i = 1, \quad & \frac{\mathbf{x}_i \cdot \mathbf{w} + b}{\| \mathbf{w} \|} > 0 \\ \forall i : y_i = -1, \quad & \frac{\mathbf{x}_i \cdot \mathbf{w} + b}{\| \mathbf{w} \|} < 0 \end{aligned} \tag{1.13}$$

This may be simplified as:

$$\forall i, \quad y_i \frac{\mathbf{x}_i \cdot \mathbf{w} + b}{\| \mathbf{w} \|} > 0 \tag{1.14}$$

Next, we require the maximum possible margin. We therefore try to maximise the Euclidean (non-oriented) distance of the nearest (support) vectors to hyperplane *H*. All these requirements may be expressed as:

$$\begin{aligned} & \max_{\mathbf{w},b} \min_i \left| \frac{\mathbf{x}_i \cdot \mathbf{w} + b}{\| \mathbf{w} \|} \right| \\ & \text{where } \forall i, \quad y_i \frac{\mathbf{x}_i \cdot \mathbf{w} + b}{\| \mathbf{w} \|} > 0 \end{aligned} \tag{1.15}$$

The number of solutions to this task remains infinite, however, since the direction of vector **w** is specified but its magnitude ||**w**|| is not. For practical reasons, the magnitude ||**w**|| should be inversely proportional to the Euclidean distance of the support vectors to hyperplane *H*:

$$\frac{1}{\| w \|} = \min_i \left| \frac{\mathbf{x}_i \cdot \mathbf{w} + b}{\| \mathbf{w} \|} \right| \tag{1.16}$$

This allows for the simplification of the support vector requirement as follows:

$$\left| \mathbf{x}_i \cdot \mathbf{w} + b \right| = 1 \tag{1.17}$$

For all of the vectors, the requirement is therefore:

$$\forall i, \quad y_i \left(\mathbf{x}_i \cdot \mathbf{w} + b \right) \geq 1 \tag{1.18}$$

This brings us to a basic statement of the optimisation problem for an SVM: If we are looking for a normal vector **w** and a parameter *b* to define the hyperplane *H* with

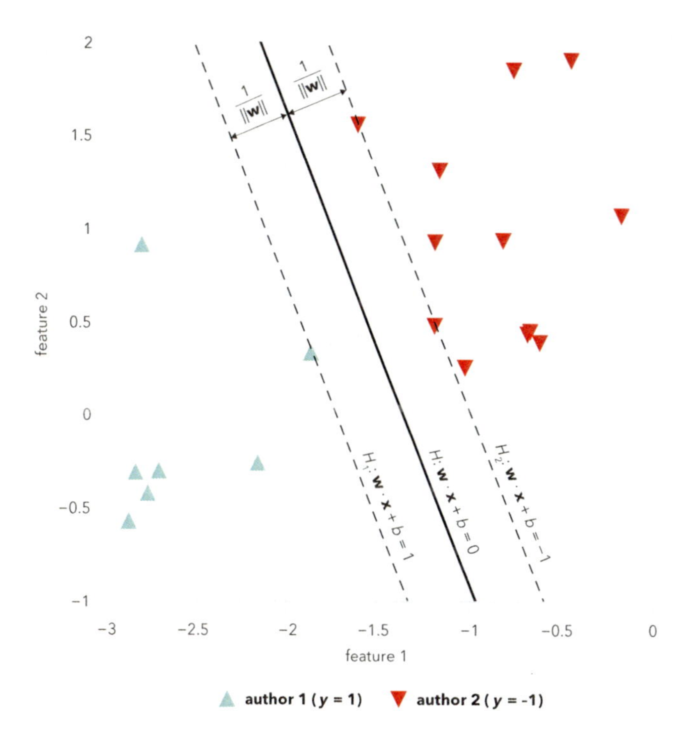

FIG. 1.5: A Support-Vector Machine.

the maximum possible margin, and if the width of that margin should be inversely proportional to the magnitude $||\mathbf{w}||$ (formula 1.16), then the solution is the minimal possible normal vector $\mathbf{w}$ which satisfies inequation 1.18 (see FIG. 1.5).

Again for practical reasons, it is not the magnitude $||\mathbf{w}||$ that we minimise but rather its square divided by two:

$$\min_{\mathbf{w},b} \frac{1}{2} \| \mathbf{w} \|^2$$
$$\text{where } \forall i, \quad y_i(\mathbf{x}_i \cdot \mathbf{w} + b) \geq 1 \tag{1.19}$$

This task is then solved by Lagrange multipliers (see, e.g. Abney 2007: 117–119).

The example above is the simplest instance of the classification of n-dimensional data. In practice, however, we are often faced with more complex issues. Those challenges include (1) linearly inseparable data and (2) the need for classification into more than two classes.

1.4.1 Linearly Inseparable Data

If there is no hyperplane that would correctly separate the classes, one of two approaches is usually employed: (1) the hyperplane condition is relaxed (the soft-margin SVM) or (2) we perform kernel transformation of the data into higher dimensions. Below I consider each of these techniques:

(1) *A soft-margin SVM* tends to be used with data with a fairly low noise level. This method relaxes the condition that each half-space must only contain vectors of the same class. Instead, a slack variable ξ is introduced to penalise vectors on the "wrong" side of the hyperplane. Here the goal is to find the hyperplane with the maximum margin and minimum "overlap" of vectors into the half-space of a different class.

For a vector $\mathbf{x}_i$ occurring in the half-space of a different class, ξ_i denotes the Euclidean distance $\mathbf{x}_i$ measured from the side of the margin defined by support vectors of its own class (H_{y_i}) and normalised by the margin width (see FIG. 1.6).

For these vectors, thus:

$$\xi_i = \frac{\left| \frac{\mathbf{w} \cdot \mathbf{x}_i + b - y_i}{\| \mathbf{w} \|} \right|}{\frac{1}{\| \mathbf{w} \|}}$$

$$\xi_i = \left| \mathbf{w} \cdot \mathbf{x}_i + b - y_i \right| \tag{1.20}$$

For other vectors $\xi_i = 0$.

The optimisation problem (formula 1.19) is therefore extended to:

$$\min_{\mathbf{w},b,\xi_i} \frac{1}{2} \|\mathbf{w}\|^2 + C \sum_{i=1}^{m} \xi_i$$

$$\text{where } \forall i, \quad y_i (\mathbf{x}_i \cdot \mathbf{w} + b) \geq 1 - \xi_i \quad \text{and} \, \xi_i \geq 0 \tag{1.21}$$

where C is the penalty parameter of the model. This determines how much it will penalise misclassifications.

(2) In *kernel transformation*, noisy linearly inseparable n-dimensional data are transformed into an (n+k)-dimensional space. In this way, they eventually become linearly separable (the "kernel trick"). As an example, we may consider the

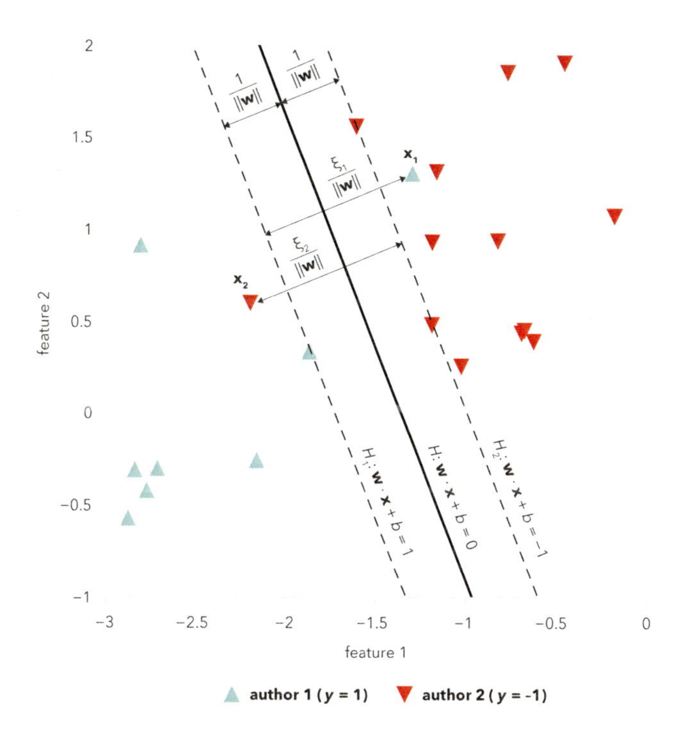

FIG. 1.6: A soft-margin SVM.

transformation of two-dimensional data (FIG. 1.7a) into a three-dimensional space (FIG. 1.7b) where each original vector $\mathbf{x} = (x_1, x_2)$ is converted into $\mathbf{x}' = (x_1, x_2, x_1^2 + x_2^2)$. Since linguistic data tend, however, to include quite a few instances per class and a very high number of dimensions, kernel transformation is not usually required.

1.4.2 Multiclass Classification

As we have seen, an SVM is inherently a binary classifier. The most common way to perform multiclass classification is therefore to split the problem into multiple binary tasks. There are two ways that this can be done: the *one-vs.-rest* strategy and the *one-vs.-one* strategy.

(1) In the *one-vs.-rest* strategy, a classification function is constructed for each class in order to separate its data from the rest of the data (k classes, thus, produce k classification functions, i.e. k hyperplanes). If only one out of all of the k classification

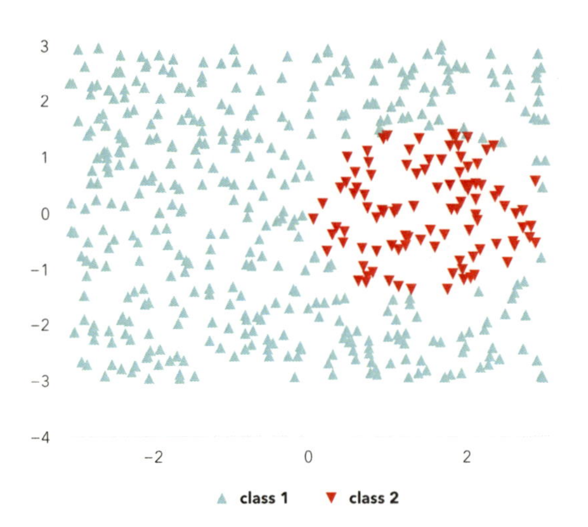

(a) Original data.

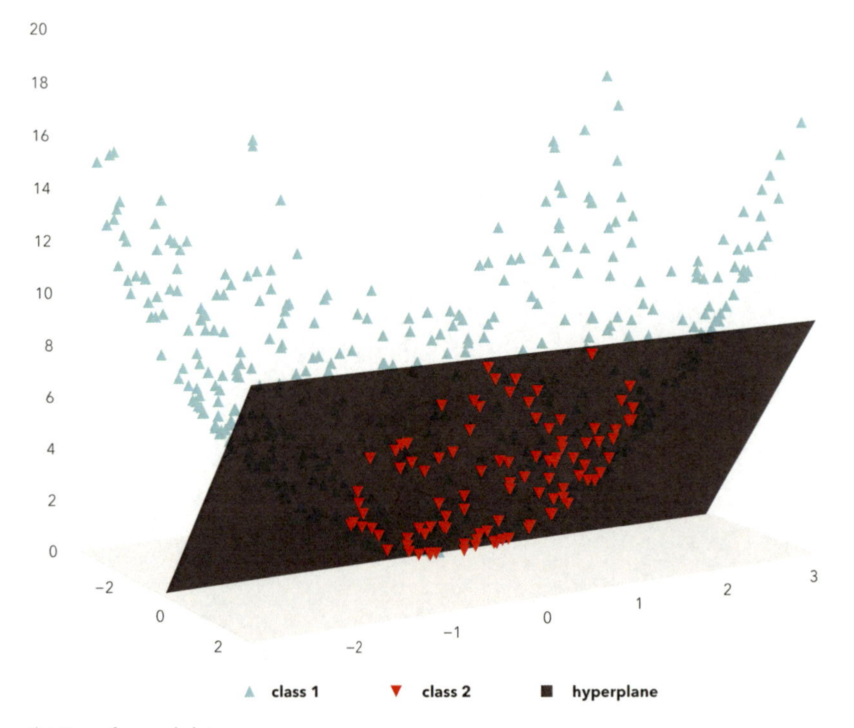

(b) Transformed data.

FIG. 1.7: Kernel transformation of linearly non-separable two-dimensional data. Transformation function: $\Phi(x_1, x_2) = (x_1, x_2, x_1^2 + x_2^2)$.

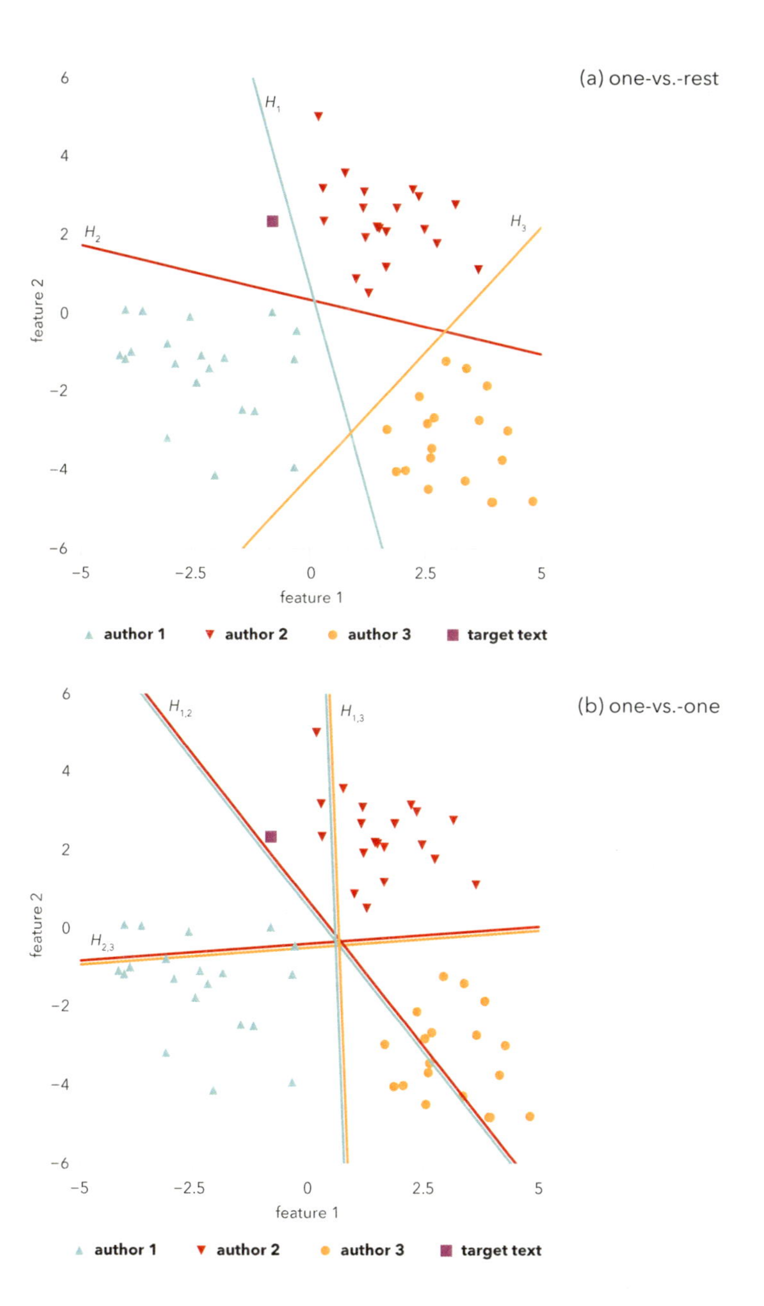

FIG. 1.8: Multiclass classification with an SVM using (a) the one-vs.-rest strategy and (b) the one-vs.-one strategy. In both cases, the target text is attributed to author 2. In case (a), hyperplane H_1 also classifies the text as author 1, but the distance to H_2 is greater. In case (b), the target is classified as author 2 by two hyperplanes ($H_{1,2}$; $H_{2,3}$) and only classified as author 1 by one hyperplane ($H_{1,3}$).

functions attributes the target text to a particular author and all the other functions ascribe it to the "rest" group, the target is simply classified as the work of that author. If many classification functions assign the target to a particular author, a decision is made based on which hyperplane is farther from the target vector. In the example given in FIG. 1.8a, the target text is, thus, attributed to author 2.

(2) In the *one-vs.-one* strategy, we construct a classification function for each pair of classes (k classes, thus, produce $\frac{k(k-1)}{2}$ classification functions). Each of these functions attributes the target text to a single author. The final verdict reflects the author selected by the most classifiers.

1.4.3 The Normal Vector as an Indicator of Feature Importance

A hyperplane constructed with an SVM has one particularly useful property: the coordinates of its normal vector can reveal the importance of particular features for the classification.

For simplicity's sake, we will remain in the two-dimensional vector space with its hyperplane (i.e. line) defined by the general equation $w_1x + w_2y + b = 0$. The normal vector $\mathbf{w} = (w_1, w_2)$ defines the slope of the line while parameter b is its vertical shift. And this slope also indicates the importance of each feature for the classification.

We can illustrate this with a real-world example. Consider a simple device placed deep in a forest that measures the shoulder height and speed of any animal passing by. Since we know that wolves and moose are the forest's only inhabitants, we want to train the device to tell them apart. Intuitively we might guess that height is a good discriminator (wolves are generally much smaller than moose) while speed is not as informative. Not only does speed vary greatly (an animal may be ambling along or running for its life), but the maximum speeds of wolves and moose also happen to be more or less the same (55 to 60 kilometres per hour). As FIG. 1.9 shows, using labelled training data for 50 wolves and 50 moose, we can distinguish reliably between the animals. As expected, the classification is done solely by height; speed is distributed more or less equally across the two animal populations, as can be seen in the histogram on the top of the chart. It is therefore completely useless as an indicator. This is also captured in the hyperplane's position parallel to the x-axis ($w_1 = 0$). In other words, we would achieve the very same level of precision if our data were one-dimensional (based on height only) and the animals were simply classified based on whether they were taller or shorter than 118.5 cm (midway between the height of the tallest wolf and that of the shortest moose).

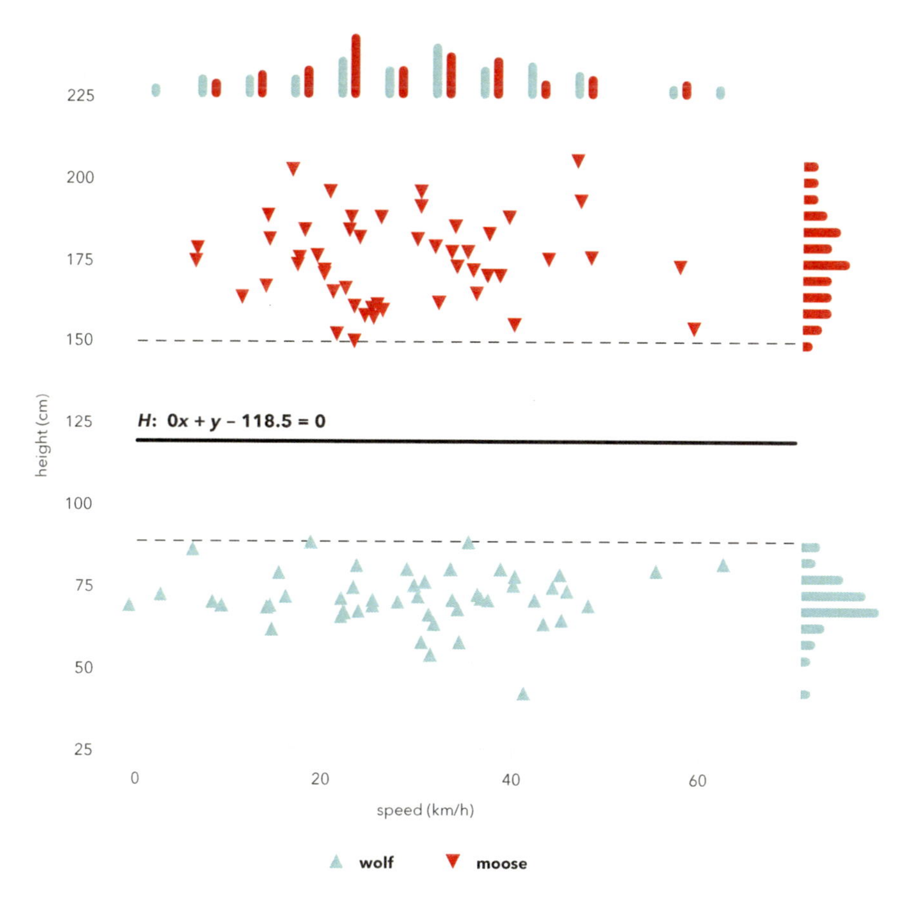

FIG. 1.9: Speed and height of wolves and moose. Artificial data.

Generally speaking, the greater the importance of a feature on the *x*-axis, the steeper the gradient of the hyperplane, and thus, the greater the $w_1 : w_2$ ratio. In FIG. 1.10a, we can see that feature 1 (*x*-axis) contributes somehow to the classification but its role is far less important than that of feature 2 (*y*-axis), i.e. $w_2 > w_1 > 0$. In FIG. 1.10b, both features contribute equally ($w_1 = w_2$). FIG. 1.10c captures the opposite situation to the one in FIG. 1.9: feature 2 has no importance and the classification is done entirely based on feature 1 ($w_2 = 0$).

We can use the same approach to interpret normal vectors of the hyperplane in spaces with more than two dimensions. This, however, only holds true for linear SVM. After kernel transformation (Section 1.4.1(2)), the relationship between a normal vector and particular features can no longer reasonably be interpreted.

(a) Feature 2 is more important than feature 1 ($w_1 < w_2$).

(b) Both features are equally important ($w_1 = w_2$).

FIG. 1.10: Feature importance. Normal vector of hyperplane: $\mathbf{w} = (w_1, w_2)$.

1.4.4 Validation

One crucial aspect of any machine learning model is its accuracy. There are several ways that accuracy can be estimated.

In the *holdout method*, we split the data into training and test sets. This split is usually done at random and at a ratio of 2:1. The training set is then used to train the model that will classify data from the test set. The share of correctly classified samples provides a general accuracy estimation.

In contrast, *k-fold cross-validation* can produce a better picture by dividing the data into k groups of equal size. Under this approach, one group is treated as the test set while the remaining $k-1$ groups are the training set. This is repeated for each group, which leads to k accuracy estimations. These results are then averaged to produce a single estimation.

When the data contain only a few samples from each class—a fairly common situation with linguistic data—*leave-one-out cross-validation* is the preferred method. In this case, the data consisting of n samples are split into $k = n$ groups. For each iteration, the model is tested on a single sample. The portion of correct classifications is used to estimate accuracy.

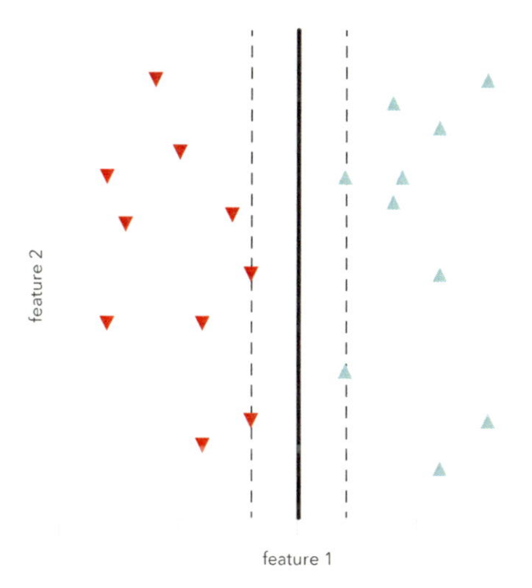

(c) Feature 2 has no importance; the classification is done solely based on feature 1 ($w_2 = 0$).

On its own, however, this accuracy estimation has only limited relevance. For a classifier to be useful, its accuracy must exceed the threshold (baseline) that could be reached by sheer guesswork. If, for example, a binary classifier has a 90%-accuracy rate for data where 90% of the samples belong to one class, it will hardly be useful in practice. A trivial classifier that always chose the most common class would achieve the very same level of accuracy. Outside of circumstances where this majority class baseline is most suitable (i.e. imbalanced datasets), the *random baseline* (RB) can help us determine the accuracy threshold. This tells us the most likely accuracy of a classifier that predicts the class at random:

$$RB = \sum_{a=1}^{N} \left(\frac{n_a}{X} \right)^2 \tag{1.22}$$

where N denotes the number of classes, X is the number of samples and n_a is the number of samples in class a.

* * *

Bringing together all of these observations, we may sum up the main benefits and drawbacks of SVM compared to Delta measures as follows:

- While SVM models give different weight to each feature (see Section 1.4.3), in Delta metrics, all these features contribute equally to the classification. An SVM is, thus, theoretically more resistant to data noise. A good illustration can be seen in FIG. 1.10c where the SVM recognises that feature 2 is irrelevant to the classification. In contrast, Delta metrics would weigh both features equally. As such, Δ and Δ_Q would misclassify the lower support vector of the class on the right of the chart since its nearest neighbour is the other class's support vector.
- On the other hand, the SVM approach requires quite a large number of samples to carry out training. If only limited samples are available for some (or all) of the candidate authors, then we may still solve the task by using the less robust Delta measures.

1.5 Versification-Based Attribution

In the previous sections, we saw that stylometry employs a wide variety of both techniques and textual features. With the exception of early studies of Shakespeare (see Section 1.1), however, stylometry has not included features from the domain of versification. Yet despite this lack of interest from mainstream stylometry, versification features were taken up in the 20th century in the studies of verse experts associated with the so-called Russian school of metrics.

In the early 1920s, for example, Boris Tomashevsky used versification to prove that the ending which Dmitry Zuev claimed to have found to Pushkin's unfinished poem "The Mermaid" in 1889 was a forgery (Tomashevsky 1923/2008). Elsewhere verse rhythm and rhyme have been used to dispute the authenticity of alleged fragments of the tenth chapter of *Eugene Onegin* (Lotman and Lotman 1986), to challenge works newly added to Alexander Iliushin's edition of Gavriil Batenkov's poems (Shapir 1997, 1998; see Section 4.2 for details) and, above all, in the extensive work of Marina Tarlinskaja on Shakespeare and his contemporaries (Tarlinskaja 1987, 2014).

Because of the isolation of these versification-based approaches, however, a gulf has opened up between mainstream stylometry with its increasingly advanced methods and these studies, which have remained bound to the simple methods of descriptive statistics.

This can be illustrated with an example from Tarlinskaja's book *Shakespeare and the Versification of English Drama, 1561–1642* (2014), which deals with the authorship of the play *Henry VIII*.

Most scholars agree that *Henry VIII* was a collaborative text in which certain sections were written by John Fletcher (the "A" part) and the remainder were the work of

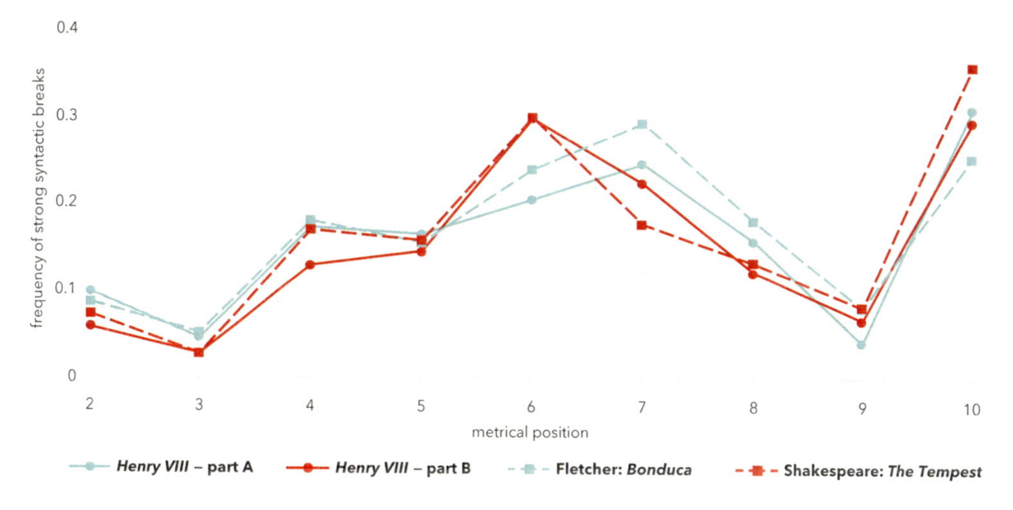

FIG. 1.11: Frequency of "strong syntactic breaks" after particular syllables (metrical positions) in Parts A and B of *Henry VIII*, Fletcher's *Bonduca* and Shakespeare's *The Tempest*. Source: Tarlinskaja 2014: table B.3.

William Shakespeare (the "B" part).[6] Tarlinskaja (2014: 140–149) sets out to support this hypothesis with versification-based evidence. She, thus, points out that the two parts have different distributions of "strong syntactic breaks".[7] She also measures the frequencies of these breaks not only in Parts A and B but also in two other plays from the same period: Fletcher's *Bonduca* and Shakespeare's *The Tempest*. She finds that within Part A, these breaks occur most frequently after the seventh syllable in a line (disregarding the line's final syllable) and that the same holds true for *Bonduca*. In contrast, in Part B and *The Tempest*, they are most common after the sixth syllable (see FIG. 1.11).

In the same way, Tarlinskaja compares the frequencies of monosyllabic words and enjambments (i.e. the lack of a "strong syntactic break") at the end of lines. Here too she discovers a significant similarity between Part A and *Bonduca* on the one hand and Part B and *The Tempest* on the other.

While these are strong and valid arguments, this analysis does not, in fact, differ substantially from Mendenhall's approach (cf. Section 1.1). Since his time, however, methods have emerged that are far more reliable and robust than the simple comparison of two measurements.

---

6 See also the attributions by Spedding and Ingram (Section 1.1).

7 "A strong syntactic break occurs, for example, at the juncture of sentences, or a sentence and a clause, [...] between the author's [speech] and direct speech, [...] or between a direct address and the rest of the utterance" (Tarlinskaja 2014: 24).

1.6 Summary

Authorship attribution, as we have seen, generally relies on the notion that authorship can be determined based on the *similarity* between the *numerical representation* of a target text and the *numerical representations* of the texts of candidate authors.

While 19th-century stylometry used simple quantifications such as word length (Mendenhall), in the years since, the field has turned to far more complex characteristics. At the same time, the understanding of *similarity* has evolved from the simple comparison of two isolated measures to multidimensional analyses and machine learning methods.

Various style markers have been taken into account for these purposes. They include the frequency of words, character *n*-grams, collocations and parts of speech, to name only a few. Nevertheless, a key aspect of the style of an important literary form—poetry—has almost completely been disregarded. While versification-based features are generally seen as author-specific, they have not been properly tested or used to attribute the authorship of poetic texts. The case for the stylometric study of versification features also has the following support:

- Most features measured in stylometry (e.g. words and *n*-grams) amount to what are known in statistics as "rare events", or more specifically, large numbers of rare events (LNRE; cf. Baayen 2001). Therefore, fairly large text samples are required. In practice, however, these are rarely available for authorship attribution studies with poetic texts. Usually only a small number of poems are concerned and not an entire collection. On the other hand, versification features are generally far more frequent. This means that they may be analysed even with significantly smaller samples.
- The vocabulary of a poetic text is not determined only by its author and genre/topic. It may also be affected by poetic metre. Forstall and Scheirer (2010), for example, found an association between metre and the frequencies of certain character *n*-grams.
- Some stylometrists have proposed combining different feature sets within a single analysis. One example might be most common words + character *n*-grams + word *n*-grams (cf. Mikros and Perifanos 2013; Eder 2011). These features are, however, already strongly correlated. Versification, on the other hand, tends to be almost entirely independent of these correlations. We may, thus, expect a combined analysis of lexicon and versification to be more powerful than one of lexicon alone.

In the following chapters, I seek to test the applicability of versification features to modern methods of authorship attribution. To begin, I explore this method with Czech, German and Spanish poetry. To the best of my knowledge, this approach has only ever been tested sporadically. Two studies, conducted with small samples of Latin poetry (Forstall, Jacobson and Scheirer 2011) and old Arabic poetry (Al-Falahi, Ramdani and Bellafkih 2017) respectively, both yielded rather unsatisfactory results. There are also some reports of research with Middle Dutch poetry (Kestemont and Haverals 2018) and Portuguese poetry (Mittmann, Pergher and dos Santos 2019). Most recently, versification features have been used with greater success to attribute the authorship of Latin poetry (Nagy 2021). Some of my own attempts to test versification-based features can also be found elsewhere (Plecháč, Bobenhausen and Hammerich 2018; Plecháč and Birnbaum 2019).

2 Versification Features

2.1 Rhythm

Since the time of Russian formalism, verse studies have distinguished between a poem's metre (i.e. the abstract pattern of each line) and its rhythm (i.e. the realisation of that metre through particular phonetic units). The relationship between strong (S) and weak (W) metrical positions and particular phonetic qualities is usually not predetermined but rather stochastic. Precisely the same metre may, thus, be achieved in very different ways in particular lines. As an example, we may consider the opening quatrain of the first canto of Karel Hynek Mácha's *Máj*, a well-known Czech narrative poem. All of the lines are written in accentual-syllabic iambic tetrameter with a strong ending (S) but the rhythmic realisation through stressed ("1") and unstressed ("0") syllables is different in each line:

	Byl pozdní večer — první máj —
rhythm:	0 1 0 1 0 1 0 1
metre:	W_1 S_2 W_3 S_4 W_5 S_6 W_7 S_8

	večerní máj — byl lásky čas.
rhythm:	1 0 0 1 0 1 0 1
metre:	W_1 S_2 W_3 S_4 W_5 S_6 W_7 S_8

	Hrdliččin zval ku lásce hlas,
rhythm:	1 0 0 1 1 0 0 1
metre:	W_1 S_2 W_3 S_4 W_5 S_6 W_7 S_8

	kde borový zaváněl háj.
rhythm:	0 1 0 0 1 0 0 1
metre:	W_1 S_2 W_3 S_4 W_5 S_6 W_7 S_8

https://doi.org/10.14712/9788024648903.3

It is widely accepted that the distribution of rhythmic patterns is not random in the works of a given author. Rather, it is an important part of their individual style. While the choice of metre is often based on general conventions with some metres reserved, for example, for a particular genre, the overall way that it is achieved (rhythmic style) may be applied as a mark of authorship.

There are two main methods of capturing rhythmic style in continental European verse studies, and both of them originate in the Russian tradition. They are (1) determining a *rhythmic profile* and (2) measuring the frequencies of *rhythmic types.*[8]

2.1.1 Rhythmic Profile

A rhythmic profile is a vector that tracks the frequency of stressed syllables in particular metrical positions. As an illustration, FIG. 2.1 presents the rhythmic profiles of all lines of iambic tetrameter with a strong ending in (1) *Máj*, (2) other works by Karel Hynek Mácha and (3)–(5) three books of poetry by a later author, Josef Václav Sládek.

FIG. 2.1 captures some important differences between the rhythmic styles of the two authors:[9]

(1) The initial W_1-position is stressed significantly more often in both Mácha samples than it is in Sládek's works.

(2) The S_2-position is stressed significantly less often in both Mácha samples than it is in Sládek's works.

(3) The line-ending S_8-position is stressed significantly more often in both Mácha samples than it is in Sládek's works.

(4) The W_3-position and W_5-position tend to be stressed slightly more often in both Mácha samples than they are in Sládek's works.

One disadvantage of the rhythmic profile method is that it completely disregards the context of particular syllables (cf. Dobritsyn 2016). FIG. 2.1 provides no information, for example, about what share of the approximately 13% of stressed syllables in the W_5-position appear in monosyllabic words:

8 These features are also known respectively as a *stress profile* and *rhythmic forms*.

9 For a thorough analysis of these differences, see, e.g. Červenka 1998; Červenka and Sgallová 1978; Jirát 1931–1932; Jakobson 1938/1995.

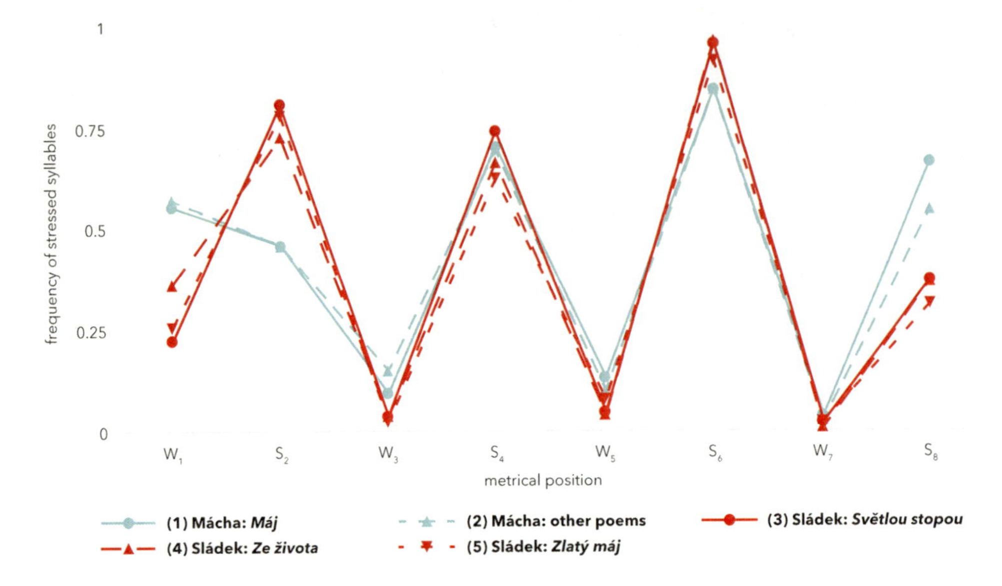

FIG. 2.1: Rhythmic profiles of all lines of iambic tetrameter with a strong ending in (1) *Máj*, (2) other works by Karel Hynek Mácha and (3)–(5) three books of poetry by a later author, Josef Václav Sládek.

	„Kde Vilém můj?" „Viz", plavec k ní
rhythm:	0 1 0 1 1 1 0 0
metre:	W_1 $S_2 W_3$ S_4 W_5 S_6 W_7 S_8
	(K. H. Mácha)

And, of course, we face the same question about the remaining share contained in polysyllabic words:

	Kde borový zaváněl háj
rhythm:	0 1 0 0 1 0 0 1
metre:	W_1 $S_2 W_3 S_4 W_5 S_6 W_7$ S_8
	(K. H. Mácha)

The most crucial problem, however, relates to so-called extrametrical syllables, i.e. cases where more than one syllable corresponds to a single metrical position. In Czech accentual-syllabic verse, these instances are rather rare:

Přistoupí strážce a lampy zář,
rhythm: 1 0 0 1 0 0 1 0 1
metre: W_0 S_1 W_1 S_2 └W_2┘ S_3 W_3 S_4
(K. H. Mácha)

They are, however, very common in other syllabic accentual traditions. In English, for instance, we find:

Those trackless deeps where many a weary sail
rhythm: 0 1 0 1 0 1 0 0 1 0 1
metre: W_0 S_1 W_1 S_2 W_2 S_3 └W_3┘ S_4 W_4 S_5
(P. B. Shelley)

The same holds true for metrical positions that are left blank (∅), or what are sometimes called "headless lines":

Stay, the King hath thrown his warder down
rhythm: ∅ 1 0 1 0 1 0 1 0 1
metre: W_0 S_1 W_1 S_2 W_2 S_3 W_3 S_4 W_4 S_5
(W. Shakespeare)

Since rhythmic profiling assumes metrical position to be a binary variable (achieved through either a stressed or unstressed syllable), it has no way to reflect these situations.

2.1.2 Rhythmic Type

The rhythmic type of a verse line describes the entire bit string that captures its rhythm. According to this approach, a poetic text can be represented based on the frequencies of its rhythmic types. TAB. 2.1 gives an example of one such representation. This is a 47-dimensional vector for the entire text of Mácha's *Máj*.

The rhythmic type method has no difficulty in resolving cases which the rhythmic profile approach cannot handle. Both extrametrical syllables (ranks 31–47, line "Přistoupí strážce…") and headless lines (ranks 31–47, line "Znovu v mdlobách…") are processed easily. Moreover, since this method does not focus on particular metrical positions but rather on entire lines, it can also be applied within systems where the

rank	rhythmic type	relative frequency	absolute frequency	example
1	10010101	0.2305	80	Večerní máj – byl lásky čas
2	01010101	0.1671	58	Byl pozdní večer – první máj
3	10010100	0.0922	32	Modré se mlhy houpají
4	01010100	0.0605	21	Já zatím hrob mu vyryji
5-6	01000100	0.0519	18	Vzdy zeleněji prosvítá
5-6	10100101	0.0519	18	Břeh je objímal kol a kol
7	01000101	0.0432	15	Tam při jezeru vížka ční
8	01001001	0.0288	10	Kde borový zaváněl háj
9-10	10011001	0.0230	8	Hrdliččin zval ku lásce hlas
9-10	10100100	0.0230	8	Dále zeleně zakvítá
			...	
31-47	100100101	0.0029	1	Přistoupí strážce a lampy zář
31-47	1010100	0.0029	1	Znovu v mdlobách umírá

TAB. 2.1: Rhythmic types of lines of iambic tetrameter with a strong ending in Karel Hynek Mácha's *Máj*.

number of positions varies (accentual verse) or where it makes no sense to distinguish them (free verse). On the other hand, the rhythmic type approach may produce rather sparse data. Some author-specific substrings may also end up being divided among a large number of less common types.

2.1.3 Rhythmic *N*-Grams

Given the limitations outlined in the previous sections, this book proposes using a method inspired by Forstall, Jacobson and Scheirer (2011) that charts a middle course. This method involves measuring the frequencies not of entire bit strings but their substrings. The latter are described here as ***rhythmic n-grams***.

From a verse line with k metrical positions, I extract all possible substrings that are of length n and start at the i-th position ($i \in \{1, 2, 3, \ldots, k - n + 1\}$). I then measure the frequencies of their rhythmic realisations. This can be illustrated by looking at the frequencies of rhythmic bigrams in Mácha's *Máj* (TAB. 2.2).

To capture the range of rhythmic variations as fully as possible, I represent the samples from my experiments with syllabic (Spanish) and accentual-syllabic (Czech) data through a combination of the frequencies of rhythmic 2-, 3- and 4-grams. In the case of the purely accentual (German) samples, I rely on the rhythmic type method for the reasons given in Section 2.1.2.

	Rhythmic realisations									
	00	**01**	**10**	**11**	**000**	**001**	**011**	**101**	**100**	**ø1**
$\mathbf{W_0S_1}$		0.4092	0.5533	0.0346						0.0029
$\mathbf{S_1W_1}$	0.4611	0.0893	0.4467			0.0029				
$\mathbf{W_1S_2}$	0.2017	0.7061	0.0836	0.0058			0.0029			
$\mathbf{S_2W_2}$	0.2104	0.0749	0.6340	0.0490				0.0029	0.0029	
$\mathbf{W_2S_3}$	0.0432	0.8012	0.1066	0.017		0.0029	0.0029			
$\mathbf{S_3W_3}$	0.1239	0.0259	0.8242	0.0086				0.0029	0.0144	
$\mathbf{W_3S_4}$	0.3083	0.6397	0.0345		0.0058	0.0086	0.0029			

TAB. 2.2: Rhythmic bigrams of lines of iambic tetrameter with a strong ending in Karel Hynek Mácha's *Máj*.

2.2 Rhyme

The peculiarities of rhyme are also generally recognised as author-specific. For my purposes, rhymes are represented as unordered pairs of the following features of both rhyming words:

(1) morphological features (for the Czech data, this refers to the first position of the Positional Tag[10] (=part of speech); for the German and Spanish data, this is the entire tag produced by the stochastic tagger *TreeTagger*[11]),
(2) word length measured by the number of syllables,
(3) number of syllables after the stressed syllable,
(4) final syllable coda,
(5) final syllable nucleus,
(6) onset of the final syllable + coda of the penultimate syllable (weak rhymes only) and
(7) nucleus of the penultimate syllable (weak rhymes only).

TAB. 2.3 breaks down the rhymes found in Johann Wolfgang Goethe's "Wandrers Nachtlied II" according to this schema:[12]

Über allen Gipfeln
Ist Ruh',
In allen Wipfeln

10 See Hajič 2004.
11 See <http://www.cis.uni-muenchen.de/~schmid/tools/ TreeTagger/>.
12 The International Phonetic Alphabet is used to represent sounds throughout this book.

	Gipfeln : Wipfeln	Ruh : du	Hauch : auch	Walde : balde
(1)	{NN, NN}	{NN, PPER}	{NN, ADV}	{NN, ADV}
(2)	{2, 2}	{1, 1}	{1, 1}	{2, 2}
(3)	{1, 1}	{0, 0}	{0, 0}	{1, 1}
(4)	{ln, ln}	{ø, ø}	{x, x}	{ø, ø}
(5)	{ə, ə}	{uː, uː}	{aʊ, aʊ}	{ə, ə}
(6)	{pf, pf}	–	–	{ld, ld}
(7)	{ɪ, ɪ}	–	–	{a, a}

TAB. 2.3: Rhymes contained in Johann Wolfgang Goethe's "Wandrers Nachtlied II".

Spürest du
Kaum einen Hauch;
Die Vögelein schweigen im Walde.
Warte nur, balde
Ruhest du auch.

The samples in my experiments are represented by the relative frequencies of these pairs within the relevant rhyme type (strong/weak ending).

2.3 Euphony

Finally, preferences for the accumulation of certain sounds or sound clusters within a short section of text (line, stanza) may also be understood as somehow author-specific. I describe this aspect of versification as *euphony*. Although there have been several attempts to capture phenomena of this kind through inferential statistics (e.g. Čech, Popescu and Altmann 2011), these approaches have always focused on only one subtype (e.g. the repetition of a sound within a single line). In my experiments in the next chapter, I use a very simple approximation of these phenomena: the samples are represented according to the frequencies of particular sounds.

3 Experiments

3.1 Data

I tested the performance of versification-based attribution on three corpora of poetic texts: *The Corpus of Czech Verse* (Plecháč 2016; Plecháč and Kolár 2015), *Metricalizer—the corpus of German Verse* (Bobenhausen and Hammerich 2015; Bobenhausen 2011) and the Spanish-language *Corpus de Sonetos del Siglo de Oro* (Navarro-Colorado, Ribes-Lafoz and Sánchez 2016; Navarro-Colorado 2015). For simplicity, these are denoted as CS, DE and ES respectively.

The general characteristics of these corpora are given in TAB. 3.1 and FIG. 3.1.

	# of authors	# of poems	# of lines	# of tokens
CS	613	80 229	2 727 632	14 923 528
DE	248	53 608	1 716 348	10 462 211
ES	52	5078	71 150	465 982

TAB. 3.1: Corpora size.

Attribution experiments clearly require the thorough tagging of all corpora. TAB. 3.2 shows that by default, only CS satisfied all of the required levels of annotation.

	CS	DE	ES
Tokenised	1	1	0
Lemmatised	1	0	0
Morphologically tagged	1	0	0
Phonetically transcribed	1	1	0
Metrically annotated	1	1	–
Stress annotated	1	1	1
Rhyme annotated	1	1	0

TAB. 3.2: Default tagging of corpora CS, DE, ES (1: tagged, 0: not tagged, –: not applicable).

https://doi.org/10.14712/9788024648903.4

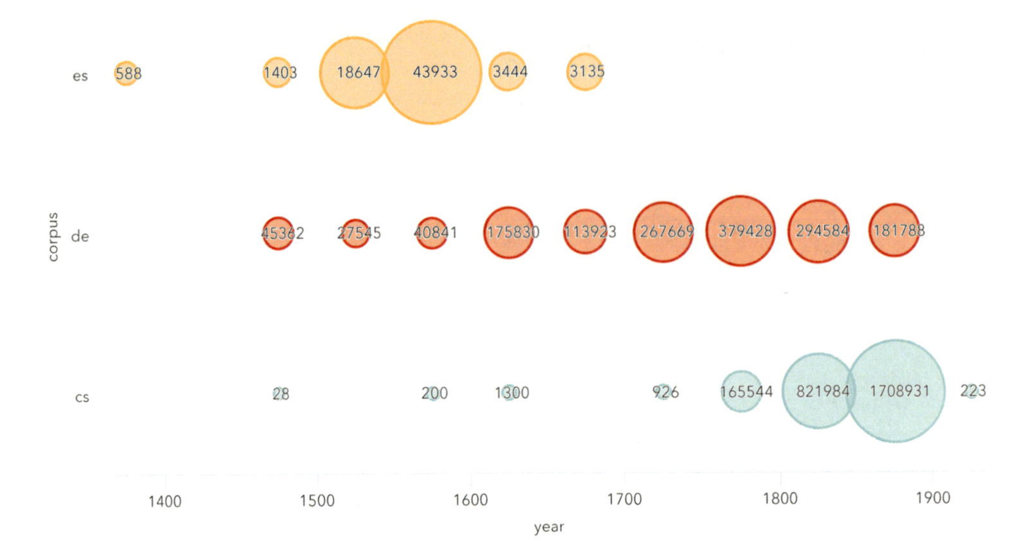

FIG. 3.1: Number of verse lines matched to the years of birth of their authors (50-year range). Circle size reflects the ratio of the given period to the total number of lines in the corpus.

It was therefore necessary to perform additional tagging. Tokenisation (ES), lemmatisation (DE, ES) and morphological tagging (DE, ES) were done with the stochastic tagger *TreeTagger* (Schmid 1994). Phonetic transcription (ES) took place via the popular TTS synthesizer *Espeak*. Rhyme recognition (ES) was done with the Python package *RhymeTagger* (Plecháč 2018).

3.1.1 Tagging Accuracy

The key issue for any automatic tagging system is its accuracy. For most of the tools used, published empirical accuracy estimations were available:

Morphological tagging, lemmatisation, tokenisation

— Spoustová et al. (2007) and Skoumalová (2011) each used a manually annotated **Czech** corpus to evaluate the morphological tagging of the combined stochastic rule-based tagger by which the CS corpus had originally been tagged. Both evaluations reported a value of **0.95** (share of correctly labelled tokens).

- Horsmann, Erbs and Zechs (2015) evaluated the morphological tagging provided by *TreeTagger* using **German** data from the *Tüba-DZ* corpus. Giesbrecht and Evert (2009) made a similar assessment using the *TIGER* corpus of newspaper texts. The author of *TreeTagger* published his own evaluation albeit based on a rather small body of texts (Schmid 1994). All of these studies reported values of approximately **0.97** (share of correctly labelled tokens).
- Göhring (2009) evaluated the morphological tagging provided by *TreeTagger* using a set of 200 manually tagged **Spanish** sentences. Instead of the portion of correctly labelled tokens, precision and recall values were reported for each tag in the tagset. Both these values achieved a micro-average of **0.94**.
- As for lemmatisation and tokenisation, these were assumed to be at least as accurate as the morphological tagging to which they are closely related in both taggers.

Metre and stress annotation

- Based on manually annotated samples, the accuracy of metrical recognition in the **CS** corpus was estimated at **0.95** (Plecháč 2016).
- Navarro-Colorado (2017) extracted a random sample of 100 sonnets from the **ES** corpus, and this was manually annotated by three subjects. The inter-annotator agreement was found to be 0.96. There was a **0.95** level of agreement of automated stress annotation between at least two of the annotators.
- For the **DE** corpus, no accuracy estimation of metre/stress annotation had been published.

Rhyme annotation

- The accuracy of *RhymeTagger* was estimated using manually annotated data in **Czech**, **English** and **French** (Plecháč 2018). Precision (P) and recall (R) were as follows: EN: P = 0.96; R = 0.88; FR: P = 0.94; R = 0.87; CS: P = 0.94; R = 0.96.

These values suggest that there was cause for optimism about the quality of the data annotation. On the other hand, the methods of evaluation differed across the corpora. Moreover, for any linguistic annotation (tokenisation, lemmatisation, morphological tagging), accuracy when tagging verse is almost certainly lower than reported owing to (1) the peculiarities of poetic speech (neologisms, word order inversions, etc.) and (2) the composition of works in older forms of the respective languages than those the tools were designed for and tested on.

For these reasons, I performed my own small-scale evaluation. I asked native speakers of each language, all of whom were professional linguists, to inspect random samples from the corpora.[13] Since the annotations captured different linguistic levels (from individual sounds to rhymes that often spanned multiple lines), three kinds of samples were extracted from each corpus:

(1) Sample for the evaluation of tokenisation, lemmatisation, morphological tagging, phonetic transcription and stress annotation (CS: 52 lines / 287 tokens / 511 syllables, DE: 55 lines / 244 tokens / 377 syllables, ES: 98 lines / 627 tokens / 1078 syllables); the CS and DE samples consisted of at least the first eight lines[14] of randomly selected poems; the ES samples consisted of seven randomly selected sonnets;
(2) Sample for the evaluation of metre (CS: 120 lines, DE: 114 lines): each sample was made up of at least the first eight lines of randomly selected poems and
(3) sample for the evaluation of rhyme (CS: 86 rhymes, DE: 97 rhymes, ES: 183 rhymes); the CS and DE samples consisted of the initial lines of randomly selected poems that were extracted so that no rhyming lines were split; the ES sample consisted of 20 randomly selected sonnets.

TAB. 3.3 and TAB. 3.4 show the portion of tags that were evaluated as being correct. For rhyme annotation, I report both *precision* (the share of tags that corresponded with actual rhymes) and *recall* (the share of actual rhymes recognised). Since morphological tagging was used solely for rhyming words (cf. Section 2.2), I report not only overall accuracy but also the accuracy for line endings alone. As all of the values exceeded 0.9, all levels of annotation accuracy were found to be sufficient for my needs.

3.1.2 Subcorpora

I extracted eight subcorpora from CS, DE and ES (CS1, CS2, CS3, DE1, DE2, DE3, ES1, ES2). In each case, the authors in the subcorpus had been born in a preselected time span. These eras were chosen based on two factors: (1) the need to provide sufficient data (see below) and (2) the desire to approximate common literary periodisations where possible (e.g. CS1 comprised authors of the Czech National Revival; CS2

13 Generous assistance was provided by Michal Kosák (Institute of Czech Literature, Czech Academy of Sciences), Michael Wögerbauer (Institute of Czech Literature, Czech Academy of Sciences), Helena Bermúdez-Sabel (Université de Lausanne) and Clara Isabel Martínez Cantón (Universidad Nacional de Educación a Distancia, Madrid).

14 The logic behind the choice of opening lines was that this would provide evaluators with sufficient context in which to judge the results of disambiguation. This was important both from the standpoint of metre (e.g. possible metrical shifts within a poem might lead an evaluator to misclassify it) and rhyme (if one rhyming line fell outside a sample, then this too might result in misclassification).

	Tokenisation	Lemmatisation	Morphological tagging		Phonetic transcription
			Overall	Line endings	
CS	1	0.9692	0.9577	0.9302	1
DE	1	0.9385	0.9590	0.9836	1
ES	1	0.9426	0.9011	0.9984	0.9936

TAB. 3.3: Accuracy estimations for tokenisation, lemmatisation, morphological tagging and phonetic transcription.

	Rhyme annotation		Stress annotation	Metrical annotation
	Precision	Recall		
CS	0.9882	0.9767	1	1
DE	1	0.9794	0.9602	1
ES	0.9800	1	0.9944	–

TAB. 3.4: Accuracy estimations for annotations of rhyme, stress and metre.

comprised the "Lumír" generation; DE3 was mainly composed of German Romantic authors).

One metre or group of closely related metres was selected for each subcorpus. The breakdown was as follows: CS1: trochaic tetrameters with both strong and weak endings (T4); CS2–3: iambic pentameter with weak endings (I5w); DE1–3: accentual verse (F); and ES1–2: hendecasyllabic verse (11σ).[15]

Each author was represented by at least 10 samples written in the relevant metre(s). Each sample consisted of 100 lines and at least 40 rhyming pairs. Multiple poems could be combined in a sample, and no poem contributed to more than one sample.

Details of the subcorpora can be seen in TAB. 3.5.

3.2 Versification-Based Attribution

In the first battery of experiments, I tested the performance of attribution based solely on versification features.

To begin, I reduced each subcorpus to 50 samples as follows: (1) five authors were randomly selected (this did not apply to CS3 and ES1, which both comprised only five authors) and (2) 10 samples were randomly selected for each author. Each sample

15 This was the only metre in the ES corpus.

Subcorpus	Metre(s)	Era of birth	# of authors	Authors (# of samples)
CS1	T4	1760-1820	9	Čelakovský, František Ladislav (12); Havelka, Matěj (13); Hněvkovský, Šebestián (11); Kulda, Beneš Metod (27); Nejedlý, Vojtěch (17); Picek, Václav Jaromír (21); Pohan, Václav Alexander (10); Tablic, Bohuslav (16); Vinařický, Karel Alois (15)
CS2	I5w	1840-1855	7	Čech, Svatopluk (13); Kvapil, František (11); Mokrý, Otokar (15); Nečas, Jan Evangelista (10); Sládek, Josef Václav (16); H. Uden (17); Vrchlický, Jaroslav (281)
CS3	I5w	1860-1870	5	Klášterský, Antonín (64); Kvapil, Jaroslav (19); Leubner, František (10); Machar, Josef Svatopluk (22); Sova, Antonín (15)
DE1	F	1650-1699	6	Brockes, Barthold Heinrich (51); Drollinger, Carl Friedrich (11); Gottsched, Johann Christoph (29); Kuhlmann, Quirinus (30); Neukirch, Benjamin (21); Tersteegen, Gerhard (25)
DE2	F	1730-1754	5	Goethe, Johann Wolfgang (46); Jacobi, Johann Georg (12); Müller, Friedrich (15); Pfeffel, Gottlieb Konrad (28); Wieland, Christoph Martin (23)
DE3	F	1760-1794	7	Bernhardi, Sophie (12); Eichendorff, Joseph von (32); Grillparzer, Franz (52); Müller, Wilhelm (16); Schenkendorf, Max von (10); Schulze, Ernst (19); Tieck, Ludwig (28)
ES1	11σ	1500-1560	5	de Acunya, Hernando (10); de Borja, Francisco (17); de Cetina, Gutierre (31); de Góngora, Luis (14); de Herrera, Fernando (39)
ES2	11σ	1561-1599	6	Argensola, Bartolome (19); de Quevedo, Francisco (63); de Rojas, Pedro Soto (15); de Tassis y Peralta, Juan (25); de Ulloa y Pereira, Luis (13); de Vega, Lope (167)

TAB. 3.5: Subcorpora details (T4: trochaic tetrameter with both strong and weak endings; I5w: iambic pentameter with weak endings; F: accentual verse; 11σ: hendecasyllabic verse).

was then represented as a vector defined by the following versification features (as described in detail in Chapter 2):

(1) frequencies of rhythmic 2-, 3- and 4-grams for syllabic and accentual syllabic verse (CS, ES); frequencies of the 100 most common rhythmic types for accentual verse (DE);
(2) frequencies of morphological, phonetic and rhythmic rhyme characteristics; and
(3) frequencies of sounds.

I opted for an SVM as a classifier using the *one-vs.-one* strategy for multiclass classification (cf. Section 1.4.2). Implementation took place through the *SVC* module of the *scikit-learn* library[16] with the following settings (cf. Section 1.4.1):

16 <https://scikit-learn.org/stable/modules/generated/sklearn.svm.SVC.html>

— *kernel = "linear"* (no kernel transformation);
— *C = 1* (default value of the penalising parameter; different settings had only a negligible impact on results).

For other parameters, default values were used.

Accuracy for each subcorpus was estimated using *leave-one-out* cross validation. As there was a fairly low number of samples per class, using standard *leave-one-out* validation might have biased the results since the actual author was only represented by nine samples in the training data while the other authors were each represented by 10 samples. To eliminate this risk, one randomly selected sample was dropped from the training data for every author besides the test sample author. This equalising approach was applied in all of the experiments described in this book, unless indicated otherwise.

To achieve more representative results, I repeated this entire process 30 times with a new random selection of both authors and samples in each iteration. The entire procedure is captured in the following code in Python:

```
'''
A dict contains authors' samples (represented by vectors):

samples = {
    'author1': [sample1, sample2, …],
    'author2': [sample1, sample2, …],
…
}
'''

import random
from sklearn.svm import SVC

classifier = SVC(kernel='linear', C=1)
n_authors = 5
n_samples = 10
n_iterations = 30

for iteration in range(n_iterations):
    selected_samples = {}
    correct_classifications = 0

    # Select 5 authors/10 samples at random
    for author in random.sample(samples.keys(), n_authors):
        selected_samples[author] = random.sample(samples[author], n_samples)

    # Cross-validation: iteratively select one sample as the test sample
    for test_author in selected_samples:
        for i,test_sample in enumerate(selected_samples[test_author]):

            # Add remaining samples of the test sample author to the training set
            X = selected_samples[test_author][:i] + selected_samples[test_author][i+1:]
            y = [test_author] * (n_samples - 1)
```

```
        # Add samples of other authors to the training set but always
        # drop one sample at random
        for a in [x for x in selected_samples if x != test_author]:
            X.extend(random.sample(selected_samples[a], n_samples - 1))
            y.extend([a] * (n_samples - 1))

        # Train the classifier and classify the test sample
        classifier.fit(X, y)
        predicted = classifier.predict([test_sample])
        if predicted[0] == test_author:
            correct_classifications += 1

print('iteration #{0}: accuracy = {1}'.format(
    iteration + 1,
    correct_classifications / (n_samples * n_authors)
))
```

The results of cross-validation are given in FIG. 3.2.[17] Since each of the 300 values significantly exceeded the *random baseline* (for five authors represented by 10 samples, each RB = 0.2; cf. Section 1.4.4), I judged versification features to be a reliable indicator of a text's authorship.

These results, however, differed greatly across the subcorpora. Generally the models fell into two groups:

(1) *Highly accurate models* (CS1–3, ES1) whose medians ranged from 0.94 to 0.96 and lower quartiles ranged from 0.90 to 0.95 and

(2) *Accurate enough models* (DE1–3, ES2) whose medians ranged from 0.74 to 0.82 and lower quartiles ranged from 0.72 to 0.78.

There are many possible reasons for these differences, but they are almost impossible to trace since machine learning generally works like a "black box" (we have access to both the input and the output but what's going on inside is difficult to interpret). However, one plausible explanation may relate to the amount of data. For authors with a large number of samples—for example, Jaroslav Vrchlický (281 samples), Lope de Vega (168 samples), Francisco de Quevedo (64 samples), Johann Wolfgang Goethe (46 samples), Barthold Heinrich Brockes (51 samples) and Franz Grillparzer (52 samples)—recognition tended to be less accurate than it was for other authors in the same subcorpus (TAB. 3.6). If we assume that the larger an author's body of work (or more precisely, the longer their career), the greater its stylistic variation, this phenomenon is quite intuitive.

17 Unless stated otherwise, all boxplots in this book have the following format: The box shows the interquartile range ($Q_{0,25}$; $Q_{0,75}$); the midway line represents the median ($Q_{0,5}$); and its value is given in the label rounded to two decimal places. Whiskers represent the minimum and maximum of the distribution.

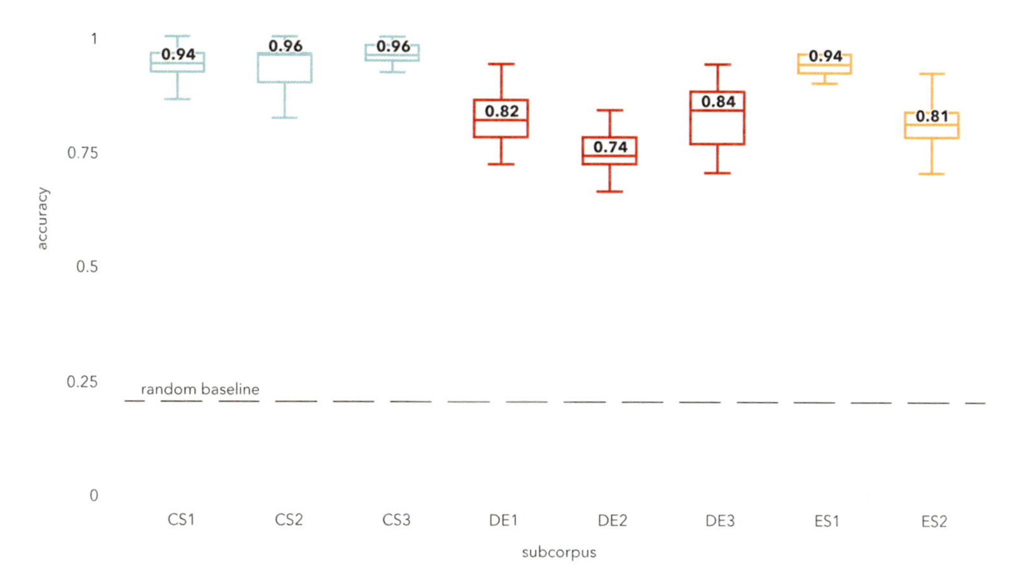

FIG. 3.2: Cross-validation results for versification-based models (30 iterations with random sampling).

The presence of two of the mentioned prolific authors in the ES2 subcorpus might help explain why its values were lower than those for ES1. In the case of the German subcorpora, we may also consider the impact of a specific type of versification (accentual verse) or a different method of rhythmic analysis (rhythmic types). Moreover a variety of cultural-historical factors may have been significant.[18] These factors are, however, beyond the scope of the present work.

3.2.1 Feature Importance

Aside from the performance differences across the subcorpora, it is also worth exploring the contribution of particular features. Failing to do this would leave open the possibility that some of the features were completely irrelevant. The option would remain that purely versification-based features yielded no information at all and the classification depended entirely on sound frequencies. In languages with a highly phonemic orthography like Czech or Spanish, this would basically mean that the

18 It may generally be assumed, for instance, that Romantic poets put more effort into individualising the rhythm of their poems than Baroque poets did.

		Čelakovský	Havelka	Hněv.	Kulda	Nejedlý	Picek	Pohan	Tablic	Vinařický
CS1	Čelakovský	**0.91**						0.06		0.01
	Havelka	0.04	**0.95**					0.01		0.02
	Hněvkovský	0.04		**0.94**		0.04		0.01	0.06	
	Kulda				**0.99**			0.01	0.01	
	Nejedlý			0.06		**0.95**		0.01	0.04	
	Picek	0.01	0.02				**1**	0.05		0.01
	Pohan	0.01	0.03					**0.83**		0.02
	Tablic				0.01	0.01			**0.89**	
	Vinařický							0.02		**0.94**
		Čech	**Kvapil**	**Mokrý**	**Nečas**	**Sládek**	**Uden**	**Vrchlický**		
CS2	Čech	**1**	0.08			0.01	0.04	0.03		
	Kvapil		**0.9**			0.01		0.05		
	Mokrý			**1**						
	Nečas				**1**	0.02				
	Sládek		0.01			**0.87**		0.04		
	Uden						**0.96**			
	Vrchlický		0.01			0.09		**0.86**		
		Klášterský	**Kvapil**	**Leub.**	**Machar**	**Sova**				
CS3	Klášterský	**0.9**	0.02							
	Kvapil	0.07	**0.97**							
	Leubner			**1**						
	Machar	0.02			**0.97**	0.03				
	Sova	0.01			0.03	**0.96**				
		de Acunya	**de Borja**	**de Cetina**	**de Góng.**	**de Herrera**				
ES1	de Acunya	**0.94**		0.08						
	de Borja		**1**		0.01					
	de Cetina	0.06		**0.92**		0.01				
	de Góngora				**0.81**					
	de Herrera				0.17	**0.99**				

		Argensola	**de Quev.**	**de Rojas**	**de Tassis**	**de Ulloa**	**de Vega**	
	Argensola	**0.8**	0.04	0.02	0.04	0.02	0.07	
	de Quevedo	0.05	**0.72**		0.16	0.01	0.06	
ES2	**de Rojas**		0.01	**0.95**			0.17	
	de Tassis y P.	0.09	0.18		**0.78**		0.02	
	de Ulloa y P.	0.04	0.04		0.01	**0.98**		
	de Vega	0.02	0.02	0.03			**0.68**	
		Brockes	**Droll.**	**Gott.**	**Kuhl.**	**Neu.**	**Terst.**	
	Brockes	**0.76**	0.06	0.1	0.04	0.05	0.09	
	Drollinger	0.07	**0.84**	0.11	0.05	0.02		
DE1	**Gottsched**	0.17	0.1	**0.77**	0.03	0.1	0.06	
	Kuhlmann				**0.88**			
	Neukirch			0.01		**0.83**		
	Tersteegen			0.01			**0.85**	
		Goethe	**Jacobi**	**Müller**	**Pfeffel**	**Wie.**		
	Goethe	**0.53**		0.07	0.01	0.05		
	Jacobi	0.22	**0.83**	0.1	0.04	0.02		
DE2	**Müller**	0.19	0.03	**0.76**	0.04	0.09		
	Pfeffel	0.03	0.13	0.01	**0.85**	0.08		
	Wieland	0.03		0.05	0.06	**0.76**		
		Bernhardi	**Eichen.**	**Grill.**	**Müller**	**Schen.**	**Schu.**	**Tieck**
	Bernhardi	**0.97**						
	Eichendorff		**0.88**	0.1	0.1	0.03	0.05	0.03
	Grillparzer			**0.7**				
DE3	**Müller**		0.01	0.03	**0.72**	0.02	0.04	0.03
	Schenkendorf		0.05	0.08	0.1	**0.89**	0.02	0.05
	Schulze	0.02	0.01	0.04	0.01		**0.82**	0.1
	Tieck	0.01	0.06	0.05	0.07	0.06	0.08	**0.79**

TAB. 3.6: Confusion matrices for versification-based models (relative counts). Rows show the author predicted by the model while columns show the actual author. Individual cells give the relative count of the relevant prediction.

classification was determined by a common stylometric indicator, that is, by character frequencies.

To explore how particular features contributed to the classification, I repeated the set of experiments described above. In lieu of cross-validation, this time all of the data were used to train the model for each of the 30 iterations with the *one-vs.-rest* strategy (each iteration, thus, constructed five hyperplanes). In this way, up to 30 hyperplanes were constructed for each author (the final number depended on how many times the author was randomly selected).

As discussed in Section 1.4.3 (formula 1.11), the separating hyperplane between two classes is defined by a normal vector $\mathbf{w}$ and a parameter b. Each iteration i in which author A occurred, thus, produced a normal vector $\mathbf{w}_{A,i} = (w_{A,i,1}, w_{A,i,2}, \ldots, w_{A,i,m})$, whose coordinates conveyed information about the importance of particular features. However, rather than the coordinates themselves, which might be either positive or negative, what mattered here was their absolute value. The importance of the j-th feature ($j \in [1,m]$) for the recognition of A in iteration i was, thus, assessed based on the value of $w_{A,i,j}$ squared. The overall importance of j to A across all N iterations was then assessed by means of a score calculated as follows:

$$s_{A,j} = \sum_{i=1}^{N} \frac{w_{A,i,j}^{2}}{N} \tag{3.1}$$

Finally, for each A, I collected the 30 features with the highest scores (i.e. the features that generally contributed most to author recognition).

As the total number of these features was in the hundreds, I regrouped them into the categories given in Chapter 2. TAB. 3.7 shows the distributions of the 30 highest-scoring features across these groups.

		r-2-gram	r-3-gram	r-4-gram	rh-pos	rh-snds	rh-stress	rh-word	snds-f
CS1	Čelakovský	0.07	0.13	0.13	0.1	**0.5**			0.07
	Havelka	0.1	0.1	0.1	0.03	**0.43**	0.07	0.07	0.1
	Hněvkovský	0.07	0.07	0.03	0.1	**0.57**	0.03		0.13
	Kulda	0.13	0.13	0.13	0.13	**0.33**			0.13
	Nejedlý	0.33	0.07	0.13	0.07	**0.33**	0.03	0.03	0.3
	Picek	0.17	0.2	**0.23**	0.1	0.2	0.03	0.03	0.03
	Pohan	0.07	0.17	0.23	0.07	**0.43**			0.03
	Tablic	0.07	0.1	0.13	0.03	**0.4**	0.13	0.1	0.03
	Vinařický	0.1	0.13	0.17	0.03	**0.23**	0.07	0.07	0.2
CS2	Čech			0.03	0.13	**0.63**	0.03	0.03	0.13
	Kvapil	0.07	0.13	0.23	0.07	**0.27**		0.03	0.2
	Mokrý	0.13	0.2	**0.3**		0.2	0.03	0.03	0.1
	Nečas	0.07	0.13	0.2	0.03	**0.33**	0.03	0.03	0.17

		r-2-gram	r-3-gram	r-4-gram	rh-pos	rh-snds	rh-stress	rh-word	snds-f
	Sládek	0.03	0.1	0.2	0.07	**0.43**	0.03	0.03	0.1
CS2	Uden	0.03	0.1	0.2	0.1	**0.37**		0.03	0.17
	Vrchlický	0	0.07	0.13	0.1	**0.47**	0.03	0.03	0.13
	Klášterský	0.2	0.2	**0.27**	0.03	0.17			0.13
	Kvapil	0.1	0.1	0.07	0.13	**0.4**		0.03	0.17
CS3	Leubner	0.13	0.13	**0.23**	0.1	**0.23**		0.07	0.1
	Machar	0.13	0.13	0.1	0.1	**0.17**	0.1	0.1	**0.17**
	Sova	0.07	0.17	**0.3**	0.07	**0.3**			0.07
	de Acunya	0.03	0.1	0.13	**0.33**	0.13			0.27
	de Borja	0.23	0.27	**0.3**		0.1			0.1
ES1	de Cetina	0.1	0.2	**0.3**	0.17	0.07			0.17
	de Góngora	0.07	0.03	0.1	**0.27**	**0.27**		0.03	0.23
	de Herrera	0.03	0.1	0.2	0.17	0.23			0.27
	Argensola			0.07	0.23	**0.4**		0.07	0.23
	de Quevedo	0.13	0.1	0.13	**0.27**	0.13		0.03	0.2
ES2	de Rojas	0.17	0.13	**0.27**	0.17	0.1			0.17
	de Tassis y P.	0.07	0.03	0.07	0.2	**0.3**		0.03	0.3
	de Ulloa y P.		0.1	**0.33**	0.17	0.1			0.17
	de Vega	0.13	0.13	0.07	**0.27**	0.2			0.2
	Brockes			0.23	**0.43**	0.23			0.03
	Drollinger			0.1	**0.37**	0.3	0.03	0.07	0.17
DE1	Gottsched			0.07	**0.5**	0.23		0.03	0.13
	Kuhlmann			**0.3**	0.2	0.27		0.07	0.2
	Neukirch			0.37	**0.5**	0.03		0.03	0.07
	Tersteegen			0.13	**0.5**	0.13	0.03	0.03	0.2
	Goethe			0.23	**0.5**	0.07	0.03		0.13
	Jacobi			**0.27**	**0.27**	**0.27**	0.03	0.03	0.17
DE2	Müller			0.3	**0.37**	0.17			0.13
	Pfeffel			0.2	**0.33**	0.17	0.17	0.03	0.13
	Wieland			**0.53**	0.33	0.03			0.03
	Bernhardi			0.3	**0.33**	0.27	0.03	0.07	0.07
	Eichendorff			0.23	**0.53**	0.13	0.03		0.03
	Grillparzer			**0.3**	**0.3**	0.2		0.03	0.13
DE3	Müller			**0.33**	**0.33**	0.2	0.03	0.07	0.07
	Schenkendorf			**0.47**	0.17	0.13		0.03	0.07
	Schulze			**0.37**	0.33	0.13		0.17	0.13
	Tieck			**0.33**	**0.33**	0.07	0.03	0.03	0.23

TAB. 3.7: Feature importance. (1–3) rhythmic *n*-grams/rhythmic types, (4) morphological characteristics of rhyme, (5) phonic composition of rhyme, (6) stress placement in rhyme, (7) word length in rhyme, (8) sound frequencies. The table shows the share of elements in these categories reflected in the 30 highest-scoring features for each author. The highest value in each row is highlighted in bold.

Among the Czech subcorpora, the phonic composition of rhymes tended to be the most prominent category. In contrast, for German works, morphological characteristics played this role, and for the Spanish subcorpora, the results were somewhere in between. Rhythmic characteristics also played an important part in all three corpora. Of the rhythmic *n*-grams (CS, ES), rhythmic tetragrams were most prominent. The significance of word length and stress placement in rhyme was fairly weak across all the subcorpora.

Concerning the stress placement in rhyme, all values were zero in both Spanish subcorpora. The explanation for this was quite simple: one constant of the Spanish hendecasyllable is that the final stress falls on the penultimate syllable:

¡Peñascos Altos, de la mar batidos,
rhythm: 0 1 0 1 0 0 0 1 0 1 0
de nubes coronadas las cabezas,
rhythm: 0 1 0 0 0 1 0 0 0 1 0
donde se rompen en diversas piezas
rhythm: 0 0 0 1 0 0 0 1 0 1 0
cristales espumosos resistidos
rhythm: 0 1 0 0 0 1 0 0 0 1 0
(Lope de Vega)

There was no exception to this rule across the ES corpus. The null variability of this stress placement on rhyming words, thus, led to its null applicability for classification. On the whole, however, none of the categories appeared dominant and none could be dismissed as irrelevant.

3.3 Comparison with Lexicon-Based Models

The goal of the second battery of experiments was to compare the performance of versification-based models with that of models based on standard stylometric features (again for simplicity, these are referred to—albeit imprecisely—as "lexicon-based" models). Through these same tests, I also assessed the performance of models combining versification-based and lexicon-based features.

3.3.1 Fine-Tuning

Before proceeding with these comparisons, it was necessary to choose a domain (words, lemmata or character *n*-grams) and the number of types of each feature to be analysed. To find the optimal solution, I first trained and cross-validated many different models and found the best-performing settings.

When fine-tuning, it is good practice to employ different datasets to the ones that will be used to measure accuracy. Since in this case, there was no need to limit the poems to any particular metre, plenty of data were available in CS and DE to build alternative subcorpora for validation (denoted here as CS' and DE'; see TAB. 3.8 for details). This unfortunately was not the case for ES where there was no option but to use ES1 and ES2 themselves for this purpose. The results for those subcorpora, thus, provide only a very general comparison.

Subcorpus	Era of birth	# of authors	# of samples
CS1'	1760-1820	32	986
CS2'	1840-1855	24	1190
CS3'	1860-1870	27	1476
DE1'	1650-1699	8	486
DE2'	1730-1754	10	598
DE3'	1760-1794	16	1295

TAB. 3.8: Validation of the subcorpora.

In training the models, I followed the design sketched above for five randomly selected authors and 10 randomly selected samples (cf. Section 3.2). Over 30 iterations, I then performed *leave-one-out* cross-validation using an SVM with the set of features below:

(1) frequencies of the *n* most common words,
(2) frequencies of the *n* most common lemmata,
(3) frequencies of the *n* most common character bigrams,
(4) frequencies of the *n* most common character trigrams and
(5) frequencies of the *n* most common character tetragrams,

where $n \in \{50, 100, 150, \ldots, 2000\}$.

The results (FIG. 3.3) confirmed a pattern observed in previous studies, namely that the relationship between the number of types analysed (n) and the attribution accuracy rose sharply, and then, after reaching a certain value, tended to stabilise (cf. Eder 2011; Rybicki-Eder 2011; Smith-Aldridge 2011). While the value appeared similar for

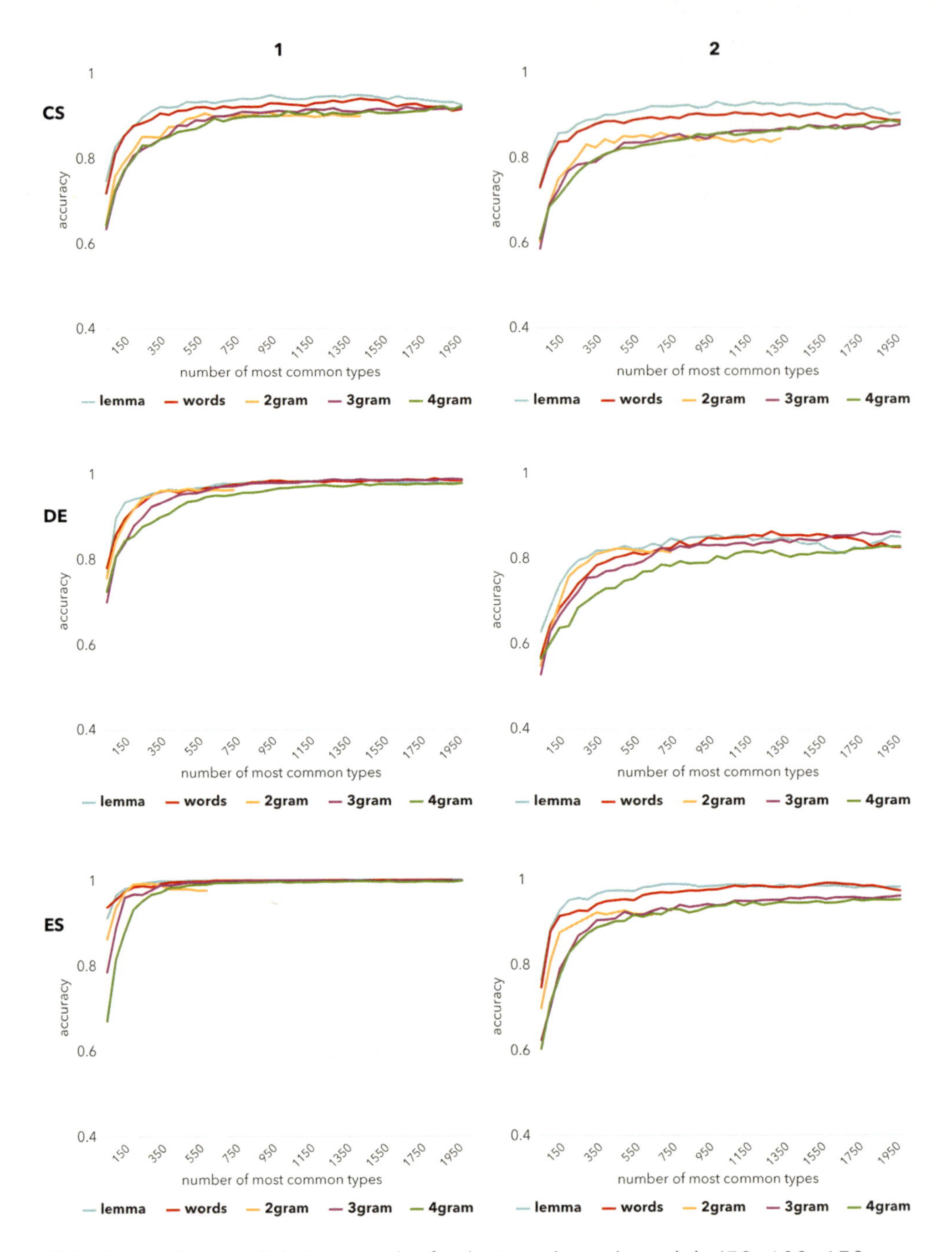

FIG. 3.3: Cross-validation results for lexicon-based models (50, 100, 150, ..., 2000 most frequent character bigrams, character trigrams, character tetragrams, lemmata and words).

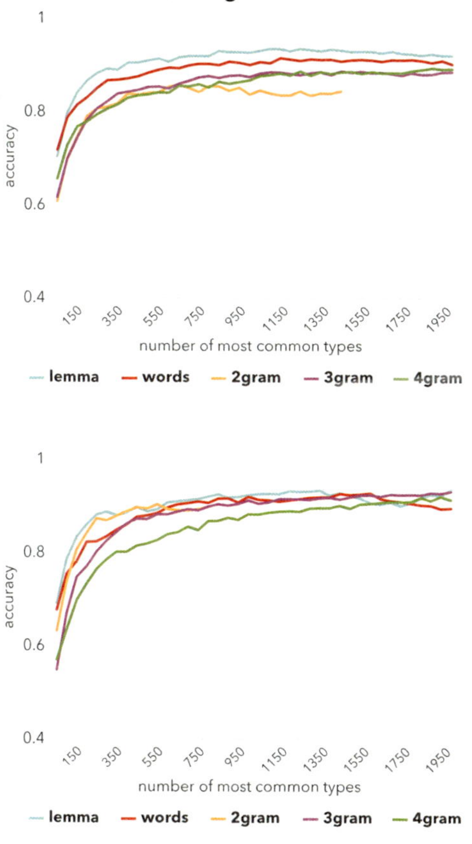

all the features within a single subcorpus, it differed vastly across the subcorpora. Although accuracy for ES1 peaked at $n \approx 200$, in the cases of CS3' and DE2', it continued to increase up to the highest values of n observed.

FIG. 3.3 also shows that across all the subcorpora, lemmata outperformed words and all of the character n-grams. In the n-gram group, character trigrams proved more accurate than both character bigrams and character tetragrams in each subcorpus.

At first glance, it may seem, then, that the most reliable models were those based on the highest values of n. However, we should be aware of the risk of overfitting: when we take a higher number of common types into account, there is more chance that the classifier will not actually recognise the peculiarities of an author's style but only respond to specific themes. An example may be found in one of the experiments I performed with the samples from Sigismund Bouška (1867–1942) and František Cajthaml-Liberté (1868–1936) where $n = 2000$. A list of the 10 most important features (lemmata) for each of these authors (TAB. 3.9) shows that the classification was based primarily on thematic differences (Catholic themes vs. working-class themes). Had this model been applied to poems on different themes, it would probably have failed to distinguish the authors.

	Bouška	**Cajthaml-Liberté**
1	svatý (holy)	práce (work)
2	boží (godly)	černý (black)
3	nebesa (heaven)	bída (poverty)
4	jaký (which)	lid (people)
5	Kristus (Christ)	chléb (bread)
6	mluvit (to speak)	zítra (tomorrow)
7	volat (to call)	dělník (workman)
8	nebeský (heavenly)	ležet (to lie)
9	otec (father)	ruch (tumult)
10	klín (lap)	již (already)

TAB. 3.9: Most important features (lemmata) for the classification of works by Sigismund Bouška and František Cajthaml-Liberté (n = 2000).

I set out to test this hypothesis with another experiment. The goal was to assess how accurately lyric poems were classified by classifiers trained with narrative poems and *vice versa*. (I assumed here that literary genre had a similar effect to theme.) For this purpose, I selected five authors from CS2' who had written narrative and lyric poems. These individuals were Svatopluk Čech, Eliška Krásnohorská, Rudolf Pokorný, Ladislav Quis and Jaroslav Vrchlický (see TAB. 3.10 for details).

Author (# of lyric samples / # of narrative samples)	**Lyric poems**	**Narrative poems**
Čech (23/20)	*Jitřní písně; Nové písně*	*Václav z Michalovic; Lešetínský kovář; Petrklíče*
Krásnohorská (37/25)	*Vlny v proudu; Letorosty*	*Vlaštovičky; Šumavský Robinson; Zvěsti a báje*
Pokorný (17/9)	*S procitlým jarem; Vlasti a svobodě*	*Mrtvá země*
Quis (11/10)	*Písničky*	*Hloupý Honza; Třešně*
Vrchlický (42/34)	*Dni a noci; Hořká jádra; È morta*	*Hilarion; Sfinx; Poutí k Eldoradu*

TAB. 3.10: Lyric samples and narrative samples selected from CS2'.

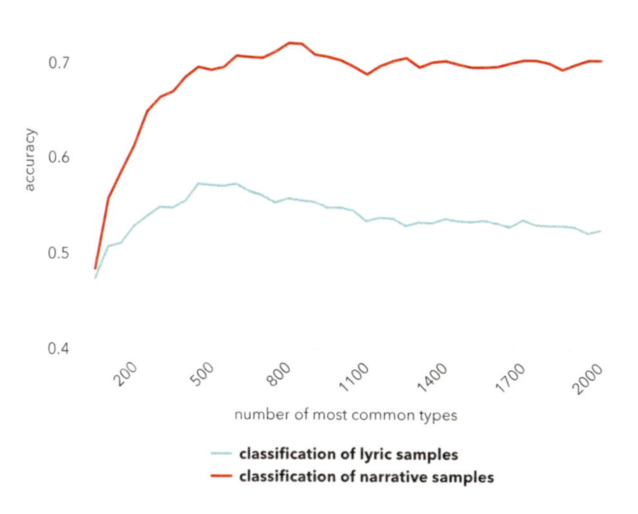

FIG. 3.4: Classification accuracy of lyric samples using models trained with narrative samples and *vice versa*.

Over 30 iterations, nine narrative samples were randomly selected for each of the five authors.[19] In each iteration, 40 different models were trained with $n \in \{50, 100, 150, \ldots, 2000\}$ and these were then used to classify nine randomly selected lyric samples by each of the authors. The entire process was repeated in order to train the models with the lyric samples and classify the narrative samples.

The results are given in FIG. 3.4. While the recognition of narrative samples generally followed the pattern seen in FIG. 3.3, the recognition of lyric samples peaked at $n = 450$ and then declined significantly. In other words, this was another case of overfitting to the training data.

On this basis, I chose the 500 most common lemmata as the optimal reference for versification-based models. At this level, accuracy had either already peaked or only limited improvements could be expected while the risk of overfitting could still be considered rather low. Notably, these 500-dimensional vectors have often been used for authorship attribution with poetic texts (e.g. Craig and Kinney 2009; Smith and Aldridge 2011). For the sake of comparison, I also included two lower levels used elsewhere including in two influential studies: $n = 150$ (Burrows 2002) and $n = 250$ (Koppel and Schler 2004).

19 Here the number of samples was made equal to that of the author with the least samples (Pokorný).

3.3.2 Results

To compare the versification-based and lemma-based models, I applied the procedure I had used with versification-based models alone. This entailed 30 iterations in which the subcorpora were each reduced to 50 samples (i.e. five authors with 10 samples each). During each iteration, I cross-validated the following:

(1) versification-based models (same feature set as in Section 3.2);
(2) lemma-based models ($n = 500$);
(3) combined models (concatenation of versification-based and lemma-based vectors).

The entire process was repeated with lemma-based models when $n = 150$ and $n = 250$.

The results are given in FIG. 3.5. They showed that:

(1) As expected (see Section 3.3.1), within lemma-based models, accuracy tended to grow as n increased.
(2) The accuracy of versification-based models was more or less stable across different samplings.
(3) In six cases (CS1 with $n = 150$, CS2 with $n \in \{150, 250\}$ and CS3 with $n \in \{150, 250, 500\}$), versification-based models outperformed lemma-based models while in the remainder, lemma-based models proved more accurate.
(4) Both versification-based and lemma-based models were outperformed by combinations of these models in the cases of CS1–3 and DE2–3; this occurred at each of the three examined levels of n (all of these differences were statistically significant at a conventional significance level $\alpha = 0.05$; see TAB. 3.11). For DE1 and ES1–ES2, however, combined models brought no improvement over lemma-based ones.

Along with the concatenation of feature spaces, I also considered how the lexicon-based model and versification-based model might work as a voting ensemble. In this scenario, there were three possible classification outputs:

(1) correct prediction (the output of both models is the same and it identifies the actual author);
(2) false prediction (the output of both models is the same and it does not identify the actual author); and
(3) ambiguous prediction (the output of one model differs from that of the other).

FIG. 3.6 shows the results of testing this approach with the same samples used in the last battery of experiments. Though this approach excluded some samples as

n	CS1	CS2	CS3	DE1	DE2	DE3	ES1	ES2
150	**$< 10^{-4}$**	**$< 10^{-4}$**	**$< 10^{-4}$**	0.3878	**$< 10^{-4}$**	**0.0013**	0.1	0.54
250	**$< 10^{-4}$**	**$< 10^{-4}$**	**$< 10^{-4}$**	0.1739	**0.0132**	**0.0347**	0.36	0.33
500	**$< 10^{-4}$**	**0.0001**	**$< 10^{-4}$**	0.3608	**0.0002**	**0.0077**	0.08	0.11

TAB. 3.11: *P*-values for the difference between lemma-based and combined models (Wilcoxon signed-rank test). Statistically significant values ($\alpha = 0.05$) appear in bold.

ambiguous, there was a significant improvement in accuracy among the samples classification of which was unequivocal (i.e. both models predicted the same author) when compared to the results of the standalone (i.e. lemma-based, versification-based and combined) models tested above (Wilcoxon signed-rank test; $\alpha = 0.05$) except in two instances. These were ES1 with $n \in \{250, 500\}$ (where there was no room to improve) and DE1 with $n = 500$.

It may be objected that an approach which throws away a significant portion of samples (in the case of DE2, up to 50%) is, in fact, useless. This is a valid concern when both models are weighted equally, but it does not apply when a lemma-based model (the type that is usually more accurate) is treated as primary and the versification-based model only serves as supplementary evidence (i.e. in case of ambiguous prediction, we let the lemma-based model decide). In other words, if a lemma-based model predicts the same author as a versification-based model, the attribution is generally more reliable than one based on lemmata only.

3.4 Summary

The results presented in this chapter show that versification features are a reliable stylometric indicator. In particular, we can draw four conclusions:

(1) The accuracy of versification-based models is significantly higher than the random baseline.
(2) Versification-based models occasionally outperform lexicon-based models.
(3) Both versification-based models and lexicon-based models are usually outperformed by models combining both feature sets.
(4) If a lexicon-based model confirms the prediction of a versification-based model, the attribution is generally more reliable than one based on lexical features alone.

FIG. 3.5: Cross-validation of models based on the 150, 250 and 500 most common lemmata (L), versification features (V) and the concatenation of both feature spaces (L ∪ V); 30 iterations with random sampling.

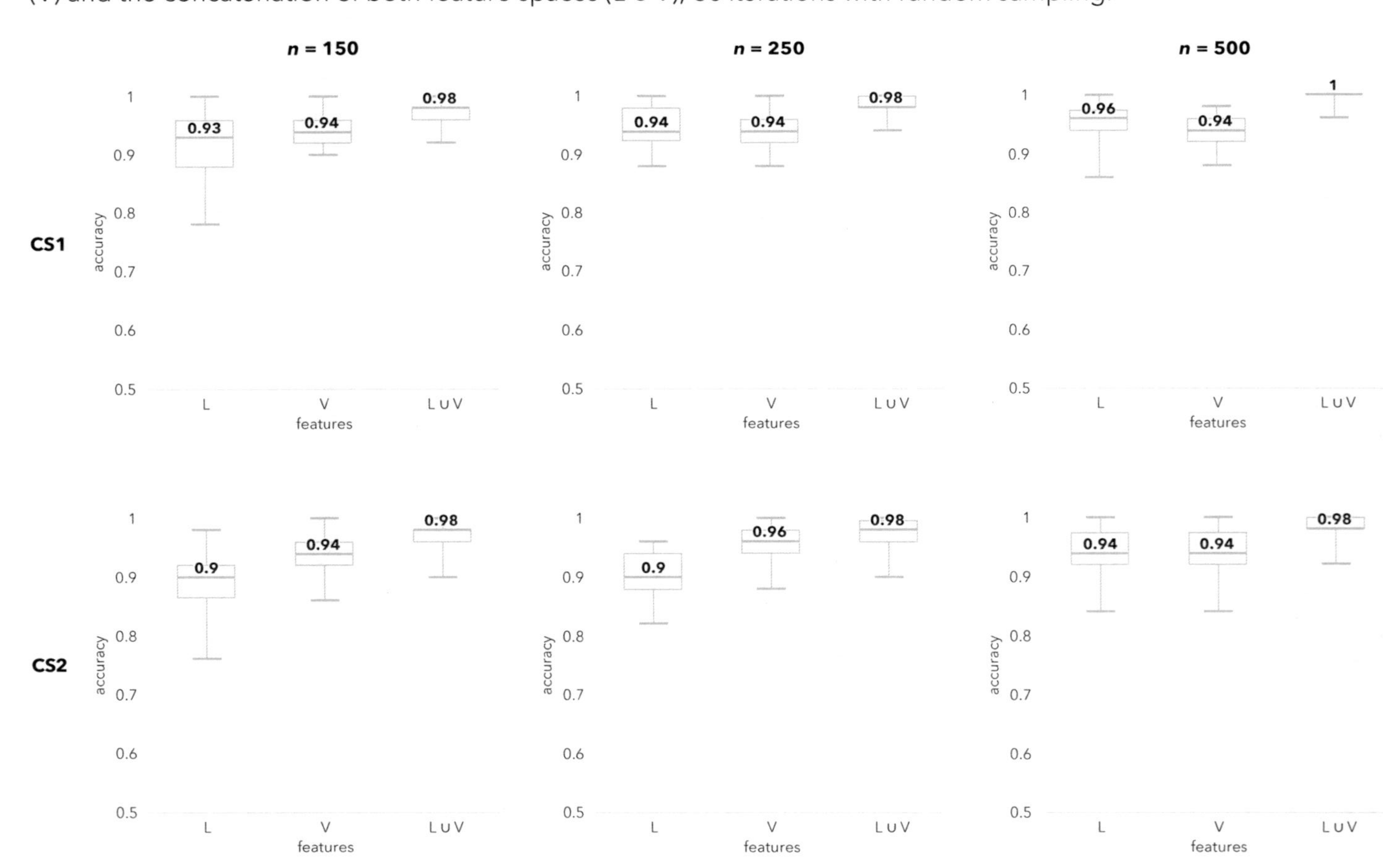

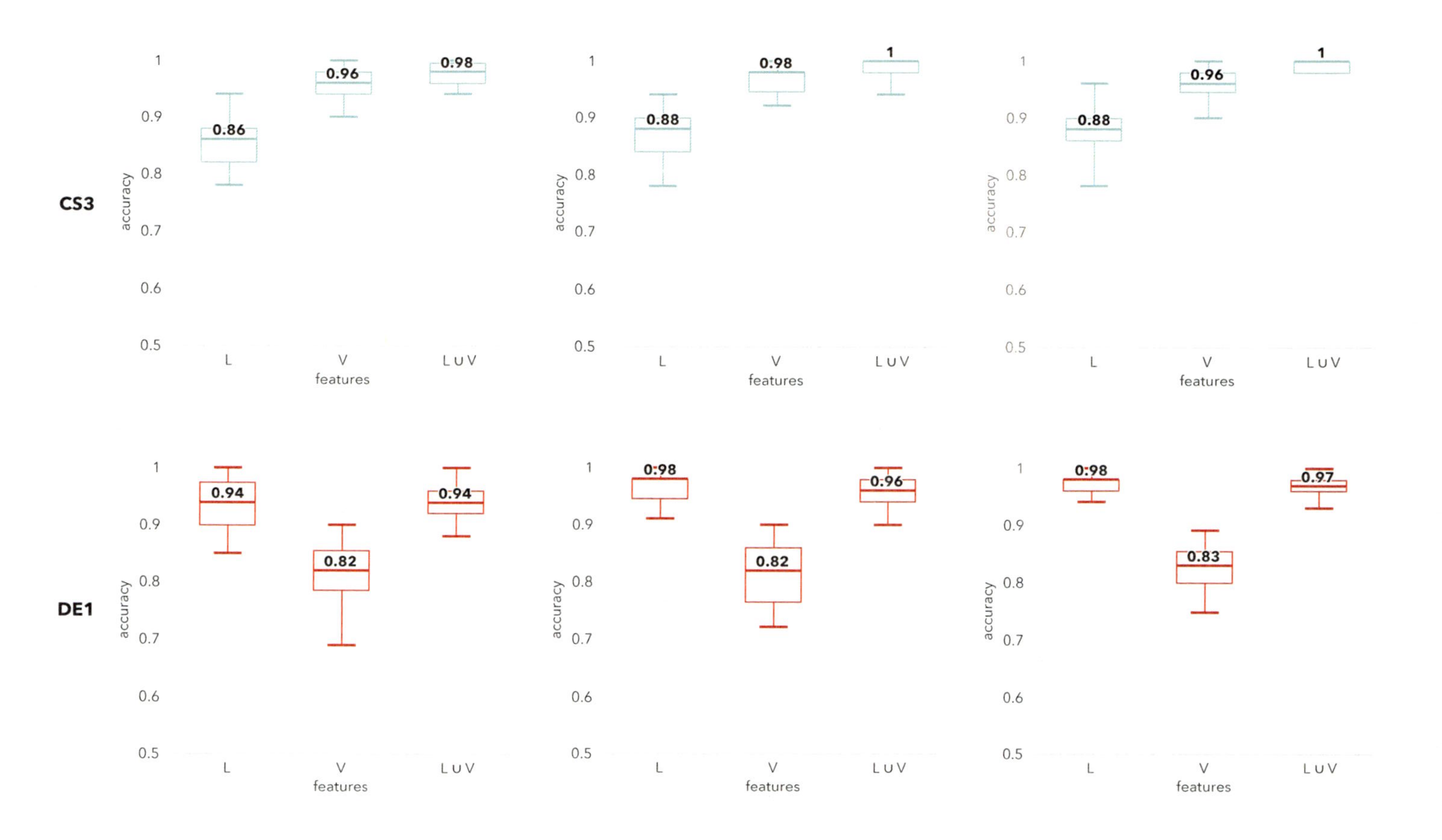
CS3
accuracy
1
0.9
0.8
0.7
0.6
0.5
0.86
0.96
0.98
0.88
0.98
1
0.88
0.96
1
L
V
L U V
features
DE1
0.94
0.82
0.94
0.98
0.82
0.96
0.98
0.83
0.97

FIG. 3.5: Cross-validation of models based on the 150, 250 and 500 most common lemmata (L), versification features (V) and the concatenation of both feature spaces (L ∪ V); 30 iterations with random sampling.

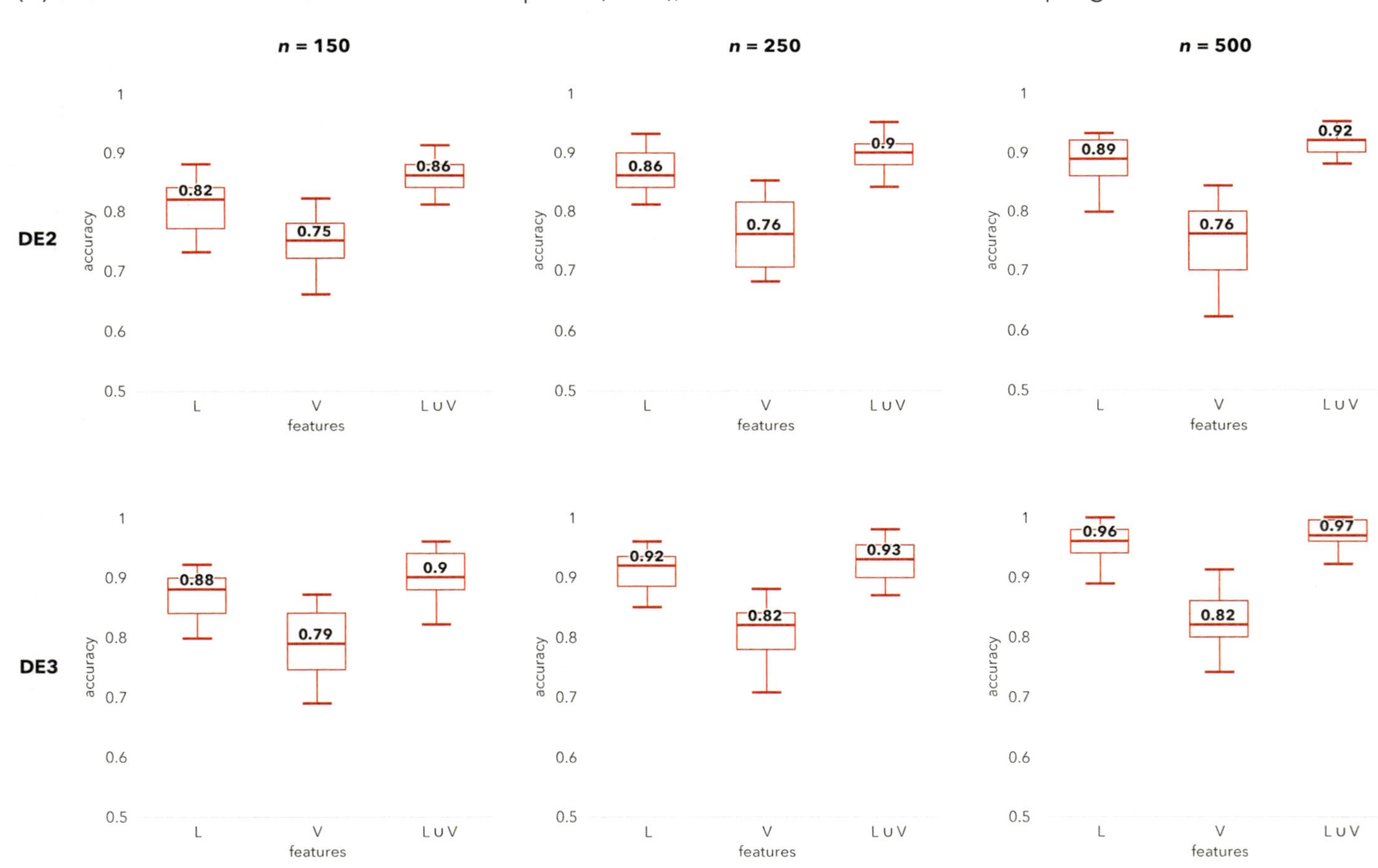

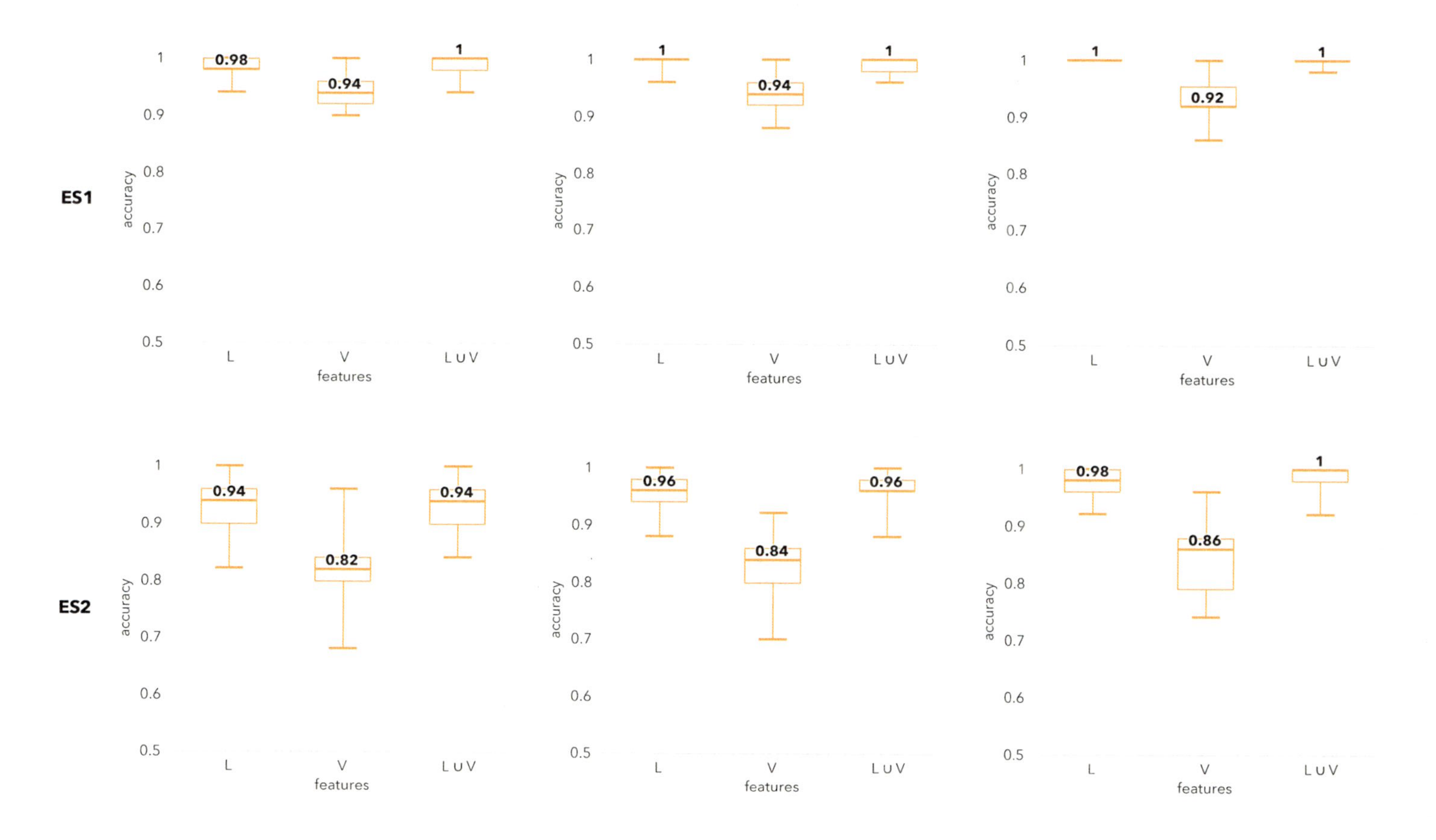
ES1
ES2
accuracy
features
L
V
L U V
1
0.9
0.8
0.7
0.6
0.5
0.98
0.94
0.92
0.96
0.84
0.82
0.86

FIG. 3.6: Frequency of ambiguous predictions (lemma-based model predicts a different author than versification-based model) per iteration; frequency of correct predictions (both models predict the same author) within all unequivocal predictions; 30 iterations with random sampling.

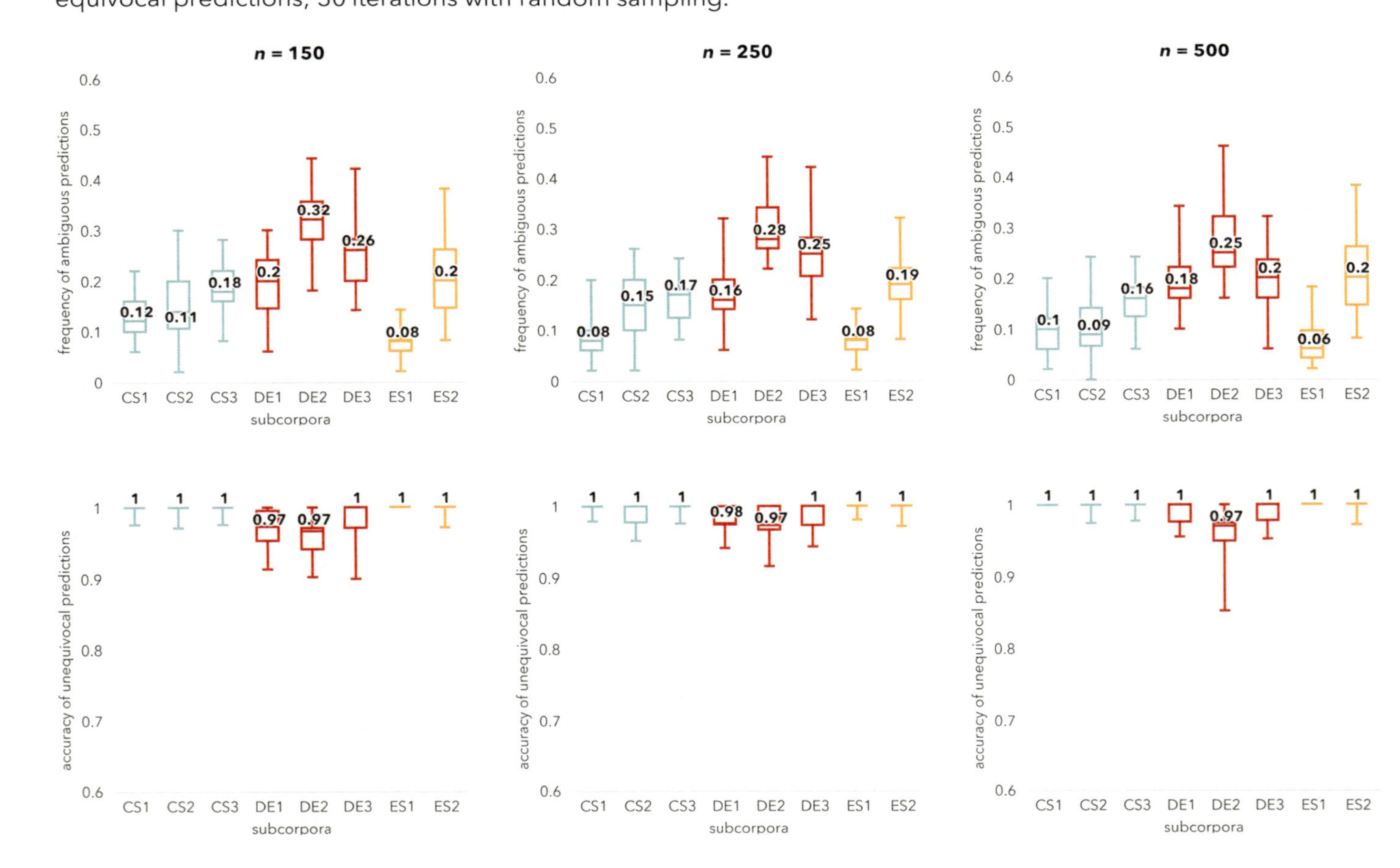

4 Applications

In this final chapter, I apply the approaches described in this book to two cases of ambiguous or disputed authorship of poetic works. These cases concern English and Russian texts respectively. In the first, I trace the relative contributions of William Shakespeare and John Fletcher to the play *The Two Noble Kinsmen*. Then, in the second, I collaborate with Artjoms Šeļa to investigate the suspected forgery of poems first published in a 1978 edition of Gavriil Batenkov's works.

4.1 *The Two Noble Kinsmen*

The play *The Two Noble Kinsmen* (*TNK*) was recorded in the Stationers' Register in 1634 and published in a quarto edition later that year. In both cases, John Fletcher and William Shakespeare were indicated as the play's authors. No manuscript has been preserved. Attempts to discern which parts were likely written by each author must therefore rely solely on intratextual indicators. Since the 19th century, researchers have found evidence at various textual levels to suggest that Shakespeare was mostly responsible for Acts 1 and 5 while Fletcher was mostly responsible for Acts 2, 3 and 4.[20] While there is not much controversy about this general picture, the authorship of certain scenes is still being debated. In what follows, I seek to contribute to this debate using a combination of versification-based and word-based models.

The case of *TNK* is closely linked to that of another play which was also supposedly co-authored by Shakespeare and Fletcher—*The Famous History of the Life of King Henry the Eight*. I have discussed the authorship of that work elsewhere (Plecháč 2020). Here I follow the design of that study and apply the same models to classify passages from *TNK*.

20 A detailed history of *TNK*'s attributions is given in Vickers 2004.

https://doi.org/10.14712/9788024648903.5

				I					II			
	P	**1**	**2**	**3**	**4**	**5**	**1**	**2**	**3**	**4**	**5**	**6**
Weber 1812	N	S	S	S	S	S	F	F	F	F	F	F
Spalding 1833	N	S	S	S	S	S	F	F	F	F	F	F
Hickson 1847	N	S	SF	S	S	S	S	F	F	F	F	F
Fleay 1874	N	S	S	S	S	S	S	F	F	F	F	F
Boyle 1882	N	M	M	M	M	M	M	F	F	F	F	F
Oliphant 1891	N	FSM	SM	SM	SM	?	S	F	F	F	F	F
Farnham 1916	N	S	S	S	S	S	F	F	N	F	F	F
Hart 1934	N	S	S	S	S	S	F	F	F	F	F	F
Oras 1953	N	S	S	S	N	N	N	F	F	F	F	F
Hoy 1962	N	S	S	S	S	S	S	F	F	F	F	F
Horton 1987	N	S	S	S	N	N	S	F	S	N	F	N
Matthews-Merriam 1993	N			S					F			
Ledger-Merriam 1994	F	S	S	S	S	?	S	F	F	F	F	?
Tarlinskaja 2014	N	S	S	S				F	F	F	F	F
Eisen et al. 2017	N	S	S	S	S	F	S	F	?	F	F	F

TAB. 4.1: Selected attributions of *TNK*. *S* denotes an attribution of the scene to Shakespeare, *F* to Fletcher and *M* to Massinger; *N* denotes an unassigned scene.

4.1.1 History and Related Works

The first attempt to provide a scene-by-scene division of *TNK* between Shakespeare and Fletcher was made by Henry Weber (1812). Based on his observations of enjambments, weak endings, unusual words and metaphors, Weber assigned all of Act 1 and most of Act 5 to Shakespeare and all of Act 2 and most of Acts 3 and 4 to Fletcher (see TAB. 4.1 for details of this and other attributions). Slightly different attributions were proposed by William Spalding (1833) and Samuel Hickson (1847), both of whom relied on observations similar to those of Weber.

An important advance came with the publication in the 1874 *Transactions of the New Shakspere Society* of three articles about the play which instead of merely observing distinctive features sought to quantify them: Frederick Gard Fleay (1874d) measured the number of weak endings and four-feet lines in particular scenes; Frederick James Furnivall (1874c) considered the number of enjambments (the stopt-line test); and John Kells Ingram (1874) applied his weak-ending test (see Section 1.1). All three articles supported Hickson's division with only one exception—Act 1, scene 2 was now assigned solely to Shakespeare.

Just a few years later, Robert Boyle (1882) presented a new theory which claimed that the "Shakespearian" parts had in fact been written by Philip Massinger or—in two cases—by

III						IV			V				
1	**2**	**3**	**4**	**5**	**6**	**1**	**2**	**3**	**1**	**2**	**3**	**4**	**E**
S	S	F	F	F	F	F	F	S	S	F	S	S	N
S	F	F	F	F	F	F	F	F	S	F	S	S	N
S	S	F	F	F	F	F	F	S	S	F	S	S	N
S	S	F	F	F	F	F	F	S	S	F	S	S	N
SM	SM	F	F	F	F	F	F	M	M	F	M	M	N
S	S	F	F	F	F	F	F	FS	FS	F	S	S	F
S	?	F	F	F	F	F	F	S	?	F	S	S	N
S	F	F	F	F	F	F	F	F	S	F	S	S	N
S	?	F	F	F	F	F	F	S	S	F	S	S	N
S	S	F	F	F	F	F	F	F	FS	F	S	S	N
S	N	F	N	?	F	?	?	S	S	?	S	S	N
		F					S			S			N
S	?	S	?	F	F	S	S	S	S	F	S	S	?
S	F	F	F	F	F	F	S		S	F	S	S	N
S	S	F	F	F	F	F	F	S	S	N	S	S	N

Shakespeare and Massinger together. Massinger's participation was also backed by Henry Oliphant (1891) although he pointed to different scenes to those named by Boyle.

Twentieth-century studies generally supported the Shakespeare–Fletcher division that preceded Boyle or else proposed only slight modifications. These works included studies of contractions (Farnham 1916), vocabulary richness (Hart 1934), line endings (Oras 1953) and spelling differences (Hoy 1962).

This Shakespeare–Fletcher split has also largely been maintained by more recent scholars. Based on a discriminant analysis of three sets of function words, Thomas Horton (1987) attributed most scenes in the play to Shakespeare or else left them undecided. Robert Matthews and Thomas Merriam (1993) classified entire acts of *TNK* using a neural network that had been familiarised with the frequencies of function words in the respective plays of Shakespeare and Fletcher. A year later, Merriam reopened the case in a study with Gerard Ledger which used a hierarchical cluster analysis based on character frequencies; this time the goal was the attribution of particular scenes (Ledger and Merriam 1994). More recently, Marina Tarlinskaja (2014) has applied a complex versification analysis using features of the kind enumerated in Section 1.5. Mark Eisen, Alejandro Riberio, Santiago Segarra and Gabriel Egan (2017) have also used word adjacency networks (Segarra, Eisen and Riberio 2013) to analyse the frequencies of collocations of selected function words in particular scenes of the play.

4.1.2 Attribution of Particular Scenes

Since the external evidence clearly pointed to Shakespeare and Fletcher's joint authorship of *TNK* and previous analyses had ruled out Massinger's participation on linguistic grounds, I limited the candidate set to Shakespeare and Fletcher. I then set out to determine the most likely author of particular scenes.

To train the models, I used four plays by Shakespeare and four plays by Fletcher that all dated roughly from the period when *TNK* was supposedly written (1613–1614). Each scene in these plays was treated as a single training sample except for those containing fewer than 100 verse lines. This gave me:

— Shakespeare: *The Tragedy of Coriolanus* (5 scenes), *The Tragedy of Cymbeline* (10 scenes), *The Winter's Tale* (7 scenes), *The Tempest* (6 scenes) and
— Fletcher: *Valentinian* (12 scenes), *Monsieur Thomas* (10 scenes), *The Woman's Prize* (14 scenes), *Bonduca* (14 scenes).[21]

Altogether there were, thus, 28 training samples for Shakespeare and 50 training samples for Fletcher.

Having established a large enough training set, I now risked employing a method that might produce rather sparse data: First I used the frequencies of particular rhythmic types to capture the rhythmic style of the data (cf. Section 2.1.2).[22] No rhyme characteristics were considered since all of the plays were written in blank verse and rhymes were, thus, only exceptional. To capture vocabulary, I relied on word frequencies since words had proven to be a more reliable indicator than lemmata at the pilot testing stage. For both rhythmic types and words, I limited the analysis to the 500 most frequent types. An SVM with a linear kernel was used as a classifier.

To estimate the model's accuracy, I performed the following cross-validation:

— To avoid overfitting—a potential risk of testing a model on scenes from the play it was trained with—I did not perform standard *k*-fold cross-validation. Instead, I classified scenes from each play using a model trained with the rest of the plays. As such, scenes from Shakespeare's *Coriolanus* were classified by a model

21 For both the training data and the text of *TNK* itself, I relied on XML versions of the first editions of the plays, as provided by the EarlyPrint project (https://drama.earlyprint.org). To eliminate spelling variation, regularised spellings (the "reg" attribute of the w-element) were used. All of Shakespeare's texts came from the First Folio (1623). All of Fletcher's texts came from the first Beaumont and Fletcher folio (1647), except for *Monsieur Thomas* for which the 1639 quarto was used. For *TNK*, I relied on the 1634 quarto edition.

22 Rhythmic annotation was provided by the Prosodic Python library (https://github.com/quadrismegistus/prosodic).

		Rhyt. type-based models	Word-based models	Combination models
Shakespeare	*Coriolanus*	1	1	1
	Cymbeline	0.997	1	1
	The Winter's Tale	1	1	1
	The Tempest	1	1	1
Fletcher	*Valentinian*	0.992	1	1
	Monsieur Thomas	1	1	1
	The Woman's Prize	1	1	1
	Bonduca	1	0.93	1

TAB. 4.2: Accuracy of authorship recognition by models based on (1) the 500 most common rhythmic types, (2) the 500 most common words and (3) 1000-dimensional vectors combining features (1) and (2). Figures show the share of correctly classified scenes over all 30 iterations.

trained with scenes from the other three plays by Shakespeare and four plays by Fletcher; 27 scenes from *Cymbeline* were classified similarly and so on.

— Since the training data were imbalanced and there was, thus, a risk of bias, I aligned the number of training samples per author using random selection.
— To obtain more representative results, the entire process was repeated 30 times with a new random selection in each iteration; this generated 30 classifications of each scene.
— To compare the attribution power of both feature subsets, cross-validation was performed not only on the combined models (500 rhythmic types ∪ 500 words) but also on the versification-based models (500 rhythmic types) and word-based models (500 words) alone.

As TAB. 4.2 shows, both versification-based and word-based models proved highly accurate in distinguishing the respective works of Shakespeare and Fletcher. The only issues with the versification-based models were one misattribution of Act 3, scene 5 of *Cymbeline* to Fletcher and two misattributions of Act 5, scene 8 of *Valentinian* to Shakespeare. In contrast, the word-based models misclassified Act 5, scene 1 of *Bonduca* in all 30 iterations. When the two feature sets were merged, however, there were no misclassifications and all models achieved 100% accuracy.

FIG. 4.1 presents the results of the application of classifiers to *TNK*. As with the training samples, testing was limited to scenes with more than 100 lines (12 out of the play's 24 scenes). Except in the case of Act 4, scene 1, there was a strong consensus among the versification-based, word-based and combined models. Significantly, their

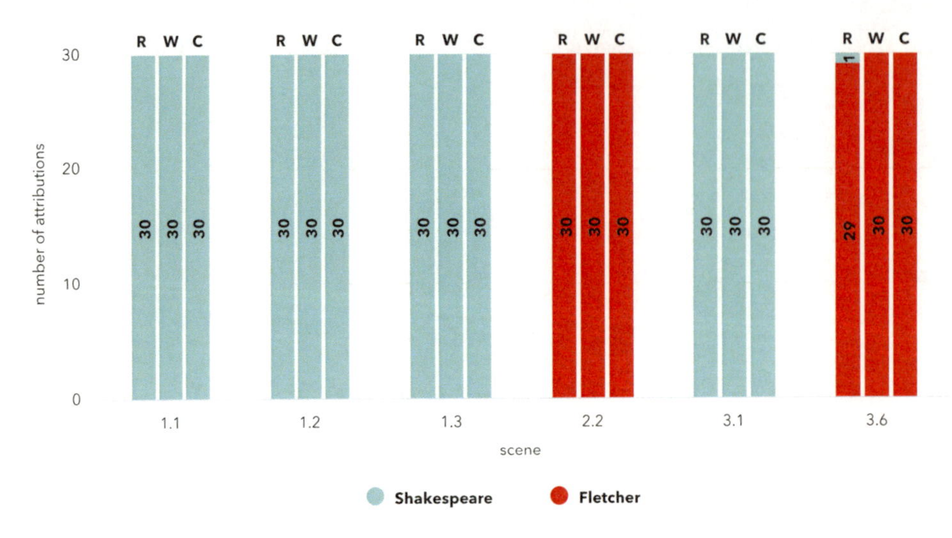

FIG. 4.1: Classification of *TNK* scenes with more than 100 lines by versification-based models (R), word-based models (W) and combined models (C). The figure shows the number of times per 30 iterations that the author was credited with a given scene.

predictions also reflected the attributions of scholars such as Fleay (1874d) and Oras (1953). Concerning Act 4, scene 1, there were mixed signals. Versification-based models unanimously assigned the scene to Shakespeare, but almost all the word-based models attributed it to Fletcher. The combined models again favoured Shakespeare.

This classification of particular scenes may have been strong evidence of the involvement of both authors. Nevertheless, since only half of *TNK*'s scenes were long enough to be classified, this approach did not allow me to estimate the overall contributions of each author. To trace authorial signals through all the versified parts of the play, I therefore proceeded with a different technique. This was *rolling attribution*, a method originally proposed by Maciej Eder (2016).

4.1.3 Rolling Attribution of *TNK*

The logic behind the rolling approach was quite simple. Instead of classifying particular scenes from *TNK* with a model trained with complete scenes from different plays, the plays in the training set were split into 100-line samples that disregarded scene divisions. Here sample 1 was lines 1–100 of the play; sample 2 was lines 101–200;

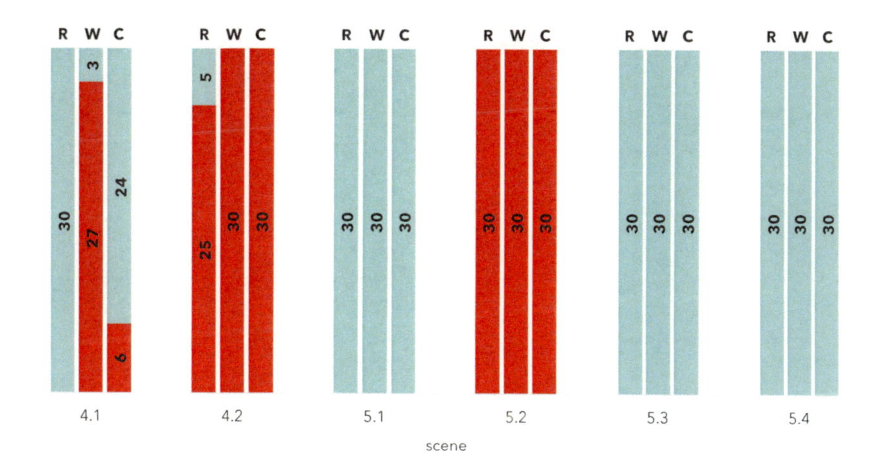

sample 3 was lines 201–300 and so on. An SVM model trained with these samples was then used to classify 100-line samples from *TNK*. To trace potential authorship shifts more precisely, the *TNK* samples were not extracted successively as the training data had been. Instead, a "rolling" window of 100 lines was established and set to advance in five-line steps (thus, sample 1: lines 1–100, sample 2: lines 6–105, sample 3: lines 11–110 and so on).

This rolling attribution scheme was first tested with the plays contained in the training set. For each play, I trained 30 models with the remaining data, having aligned the number of training samples by random selection in each iteration. To enhance authorship detection even further, I avoided binary classification (author = Shakespeare | author = Fletcher) and instead transformed the output into a probability distribution between the two authors via Platt scaling (Platt 1999).

I focused here not on the complete samples but rather on the successive series of five lines. With a sample size of 100 lines, a "step" set to five lines and 30 different models, each five-line series in *TNK* (except for the initial 19 and final 19 series) was classified 600 times—that is, 30 times within 20 different samples. I averaged out the probabilities obtained from the different models and samples for these series.

FIG. 4.2 shows the results for the combined models as well as those for the versification-based models and word-based models on their own. The versification-based models produced several misclassifications. In particular, 15 series from Act 4, scene 1 and two series from Act 5, scene 8 of *Valentinian* were misattributed to Shakespeare. The probabilities of Shakespearean and Fletcherian authorship also came close in a couple of series in Act 2 scene 1 of *Bonduca* although Shakespeare's values remained slightly higher. Nevertheless, since there were only 17 misclassifications out of a total

FIG. 4.2: Rolling attribution of four plays by Shakespeare and four plays by Fletcher based on the 500 most common rhythmic types and the 500 most common words (upper = *P*(Shakespeare), lower = *P*(Fletcher)). Vertical lines indicate scene breaks. Dotted lines show the results of rolling attribution based solely on the 500 most common rhythmic types. Dashed lines show the results of rolling attribution based solely on the 500 most common words.

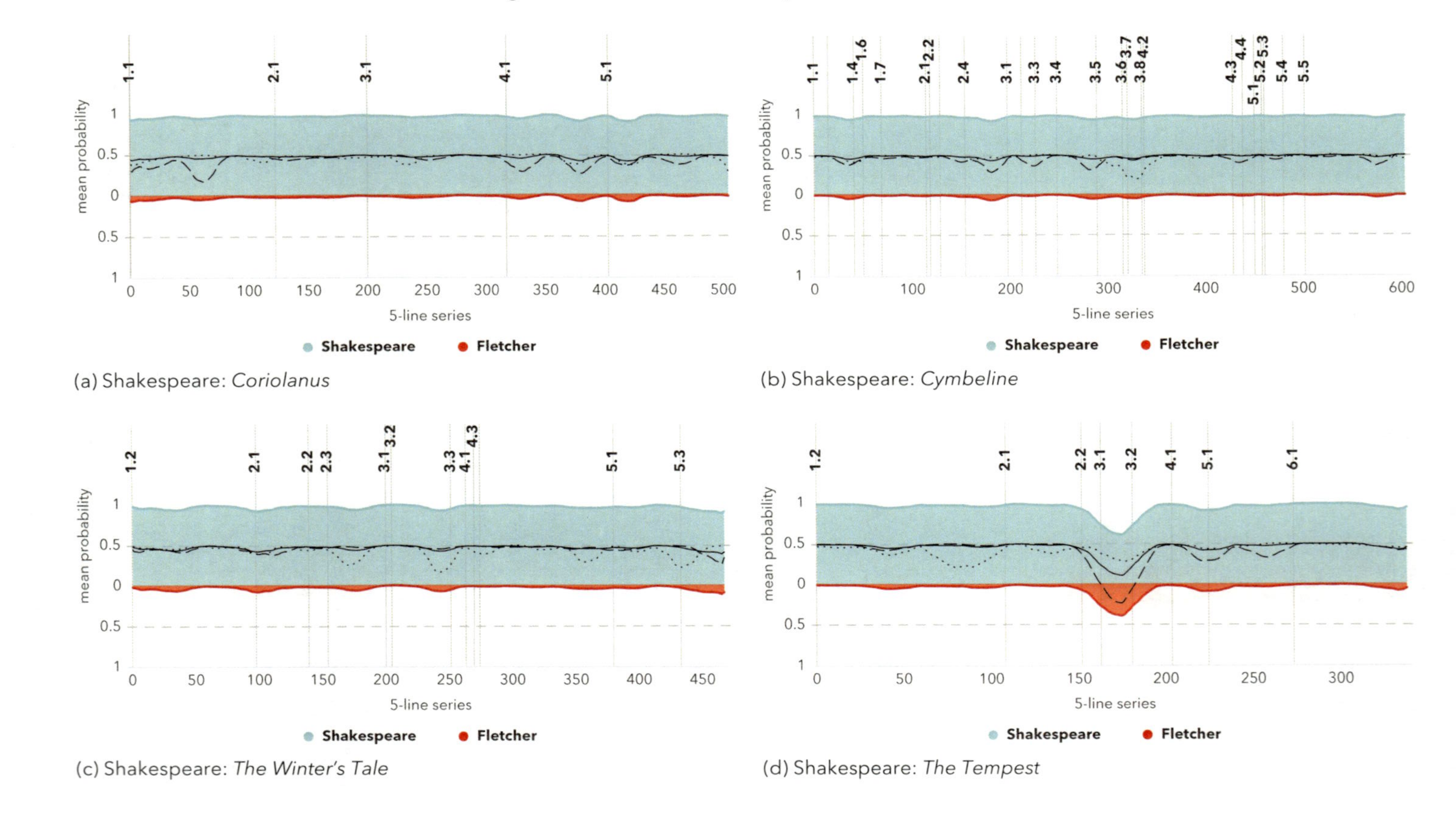

(a) Shakespeare: *Coriolanus*

(b) Shakespeare: *Cymbeline*

(c) Shakespeare: *The Winter's Tale*

(d) Shakespeare: *The Tempest*

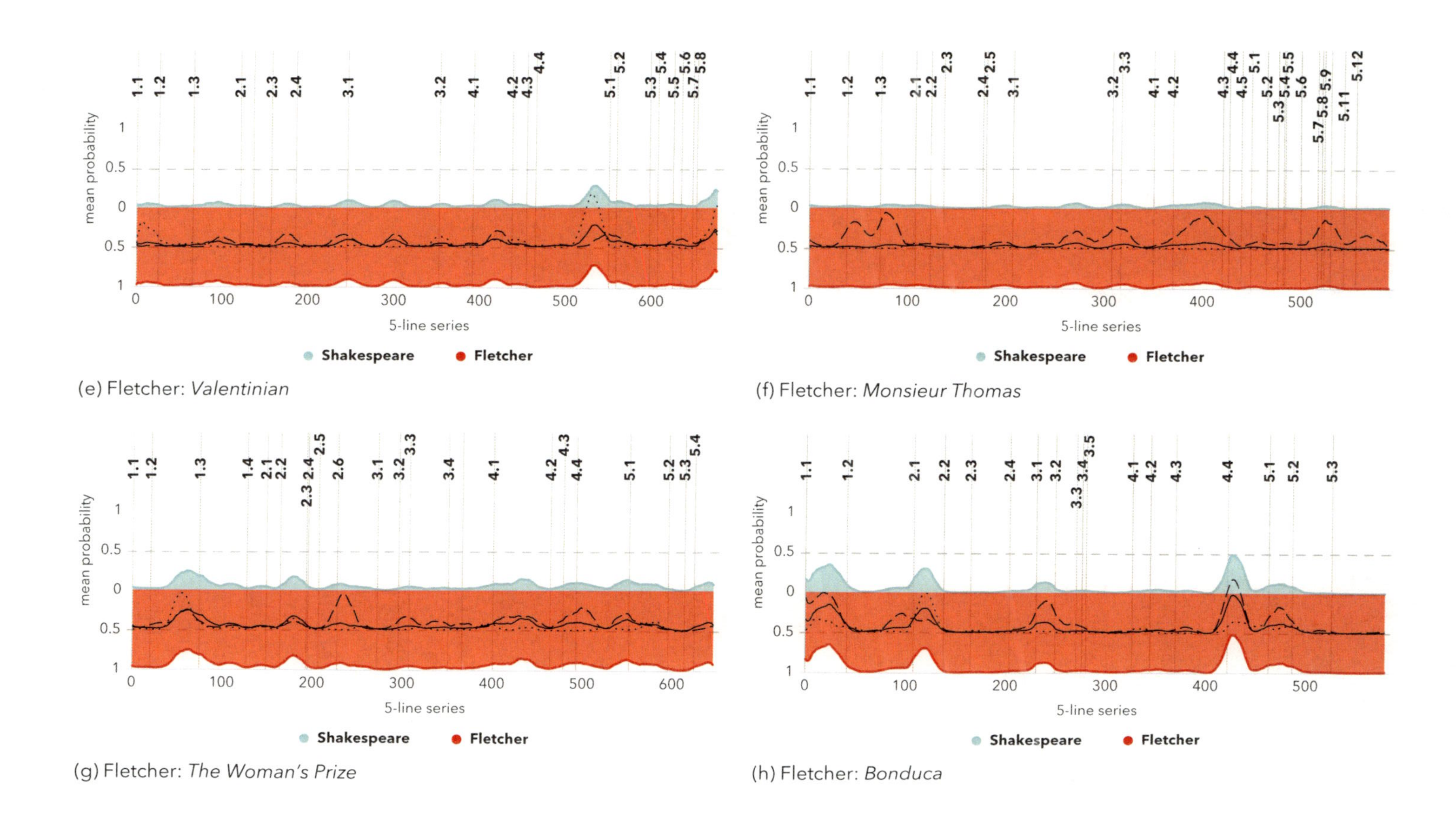

(e) Fletcher: *Valentinian*

(f) Fletcher: *Monsieur Thomas*

(g) Fletcher: *The Woman's Prize*

(h) Fletcher: *Bonduca*

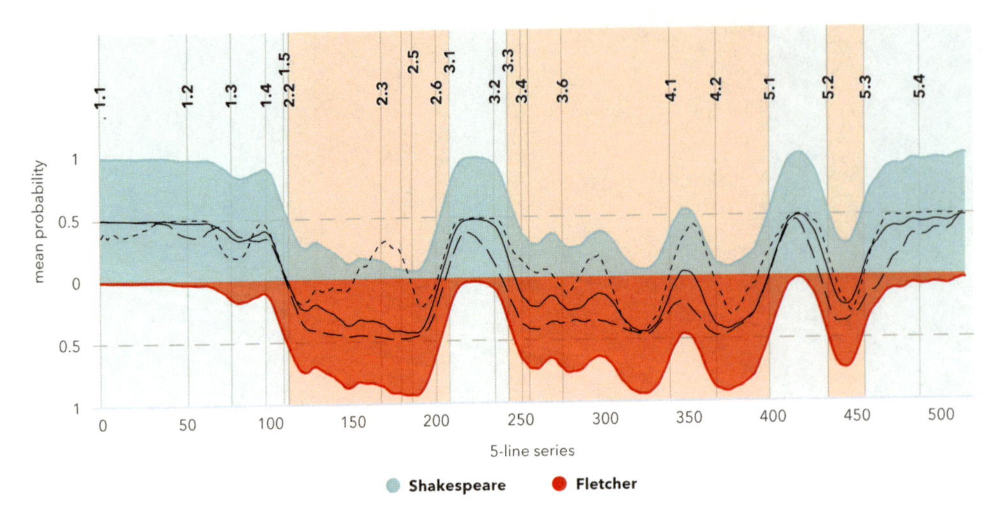

FIG. 4.3: Rolling attribution of *TNK* based on the 500 most common rhythmic types and the 500 most common words (upper = *P*(Shakespeare), lower = *P*(Fletcher)). Vertical lines indicate scene breaks. Dotted lines show the results of rolling attribution based solely on the 500 most common rhythmic types. Dashed lines show the results of rolling attribution based solely on the 500 most common words. The background colour indicates the author to whom the scene is usually credited.

4412 series, the overall accuracy rate was high at 0.996. Word-based models also gave rise to misclassifications: in Act 3, scene 1 of *The Tempest*, 20 series were misattributed to Fletcher while 14 series in Act 4, scene 4 of *Bonduca* were wrongly assigned to Shakespeare; Shakespeare and Fletcher were again weighted similarly for Act 1, scene 1 of *Bonduca*. Total accuracy was, thus, 0.992.

Crucially, all of these outlying results were absorbed and no series was misclassified when the feature sets were merged in the combined model.

Having verified the performance of the models, I turned to the evaluation of *TNK* itself. FIG. 4.3 gives the results of the rolling attribution of the play using models trained with all eight plays in the training set.

There were some remarkable discrepancies between the results of the versification-based and word-based models. This applied especially to the following sequences of *TNK*: from the end of Act 2, scene 2 to the end of Act 2, scene 4; from Act 3, scene 3 to Act 3, scene 5; and during Act 3, scene 6 and Act 4, scene 1. Interestingly enough, these were not controversial scenes where such behaviour might be expected but rather parts of play whose attribution had been stable for the last two centuries (cf. TAB. 4.1). We may, however, be guided here by the combined model, which had proven most reliable and produced somewhat consistent results with *TNK* as well.

Based on these findings, it was highly probable that Shakespeare was the author of all of Act 1 and Fletcher was the author of all of Act 2. Indeed, the shift in authorship seemed to coincide with the break between these examined parts. (Significantly, Act 2, scene 1, which is usually assigned to Shakespeare, was excluded from the data because it was written in prose.) The models strongly favoured Shakespeare again in Act 3, scenes 1 and 2 (or, more precisely, from the end of Act 2, scene 6 to the start of Act 3, scene 3). For the remainder of Act 3 and Act 4 (excluding the prose text of Act 4, scene 3), Fletcher was the preference for all but nine series in Act 4, scene 1. As the final act opened, the likelihood of Shakespearean authorship rose sharply again and it remained high until the end of the play except in Act 5, scene 2 where Fletcher was the clear choice of the models. Again the authorial changes seemed to match scene breaks precisely.

All in all, then, the models strongly supported Shakespeare as the author of Act 1, scenes 1–5; Act 3, scenes 1–2; and Act 5, scenes 1 and 3–4. Similarly, they backed Fletcher as the author of Act 2, scenes 2–6; Act 3, scenes 3–6; Act 4, scene 2; and Act 5, scene 2. The authorship of Act 4, scene 1 remained uncertain. Notably, these results confirmed the attributions proposed by Fleay (1874d) and Oras (1953). Given that these scholars and others have provided (mostly orthogonal) evidence for Fletcher's authorship of Act 4, scene 1, it is tempting to lean towards the same conclusion.

4.1.4 Summary

Combined versification- and word-based models turned out to be highly accurate in distinguishing the work of Shakespeare from that of Fletcher. In the case of *The Two Noble Kinsmen,* the application of these models to particular scenes—especially when paired with rolling attribution—supported what may be called the orthodox division of the play.

These findings clearly testify to the efforts of the brilliant scholars who were able decades or more ago to identify the most salient features of the two authors' styles without the aid of any machines or feature selection algorithms. Instead they relied solely on thorough study of the texts in question. The features they pinpointed—for instance, the frequencies of *'em / them* (Thorndike 1901), *th'*, *i'* (Farnham 1916) and *doth* and *ye* (Hoy 1962)—all rank among those found to be most important for the classification.[23] This is also true of line endings (Fleay 1874d). Common strong ending rhythmic types such as 0101010101 (0 = unstressed syllable, 1 = stressed syllable), 0101000101 and 0100010101 were among the most strongly-weighted positive (Shakespearian) features. Similarly, common W-position-terminated rhythmic types such as 01010101010 and 10010100010 appeared among the most strongly-weighted negative (Fletcherian) features.

4.2 The Case of (Pseudo-)Batenkov: Towards a Formal Proof of Literary Forgery *(co-authored by Artjoms Šeļa)*

In 1978, a scholarly monograph about the poetry of G. S. Batenkov (1793–1863) was published in Moscow under the title *Poezia dekabrista Gavriila Stepanovicha Batenkova* (Iliushin 1978). Its author was A. A. Iliushin. What appeared to be a complete collection of Batenkov's poems was appended to the volume.

Batenkov, a Russian officer and poet, had fought in the Napoleonic wars and later worked as an engineer and policymaker. His eclectic ideological interests, which ranged from freemasonry and Christian mysticism to political reform, led him to join secret societies and eventually become associated with the Decembrist revolt of 1825. This effectively ended his life as a free citizen of the Empire. He was sentenced to 25 years of solitary confinement in the Peter and Paul Fortress in Saint Petersburg and, after serving 20 years, exiled to Siberia.

Iliushin, who was both the author of the monograph and the editor of the appendix, was a Russian versification scholar and poetry specialist. He also wrote poetry himself and was known in academic circles for his literary games and imitations. The majority of Batenkov's late poems (i.e. those written after his release from prison) appeared for the very first time in this collection. There was, however, one major problem: the source of these texts was inaccessible and their origins unverifiable. Iliushin himself referred to a manuscript that was listed as lost in the archives (Shapir 2000).

For 20 years, no one publicly questioned the authenticity of these poems. This all changed when the scholar M. I. Shapir published a series of studies in the late 1990s that showed that there were indeed grounds for doubt. Shapir (1997, 1998) conducted

23 This appraisal is based on the mean value for feature importance in 30 combined models trained with 100-line samples taken from the training set (four plays by Shakespeare, four plays by Fletcher).

an extensive quantitative analysis of the poems in the controversial section of Batenkov's work (we refer to these texts as the "disputed poems"). To this end, he meticulously examined every linguistic level—prosody, metrics, morphology, syntax and semantics—and pointed out many significant differences between these texts and Batenkov's known works. Among the issues Shapir observed in the disputed poems were their abundance of inexact rhymes, overly archaic morphology, discrepancies in the use of pronouns and conjunctions and some possible anachronisms. To date, his analysis remains one of the most impressive non-computational authorship attribution studies of Russian poetry.

This research convinced many scholars that the disputed poems were in fact forgeries (Gasparov and Tarlinskaja 2008; Tarlinskaja 2014). Indeed, in the years since, this consensus has become so strong that the editors of a recently published collection of Iliushin's original poems did not hesitate to include all of the disputed poems in the volume (Iliushin 2020). However, this interpretation is at odds with Shapir's own conclusion: having uncovered significant differences at some textual levels but striking similarities at others, he judged that there was not enough evidence to draw any conclusions about the origins of the disputed poems. This reasoning led Shapir to an important generalisation about the limitations of using formal and linguistic methods to determine authorship. If, as he argued, we cannot trace the identity of an author based on various levels of linguistic features, then the concept of the "author" who makes linguistic choices that are unique and recognizable is nothing more than a scholarly construct.

From a modern-day perspective, Shapir's strong statements lack methodological support. Compared with other scholars who have used versification features for authorship attribution (Tomashevsky 1923/2008; Lotman and Lotman 1986; Tarlinskaja 2014), Shapir dramatically increased the number of textual levels under investigation. Nevertheless, his analysis remained univariate: all of the levels were treated in isolation and the features were compared one by one. It might be said, then, that Shapir's inquiry was multivariate in scope but he lacked the tools to deal with multivariate and seemingly contradictory signals. As a result, he could not estimate the compound authorial signal in either Batenkov's known works or the disputed poems. Key questions went unaddressed: How important were the differences in the frequency of inexact rhymes or function words compared, say, with similarities in the rhythmic structure of iambic tetrameter and use of formulae?

In the final part of this book, we return to this question that Shapir left unsolved. Our aim is to reach a more definitive conclusion about the authorship of the disputed poems using a multivariate approach that combines lexical and versification features. We break the problem down into the following experiments:

— We first test the general performance of our approach using 19th-century Russian poetry data.
— We then formulate the task as a *verification* problem. The goal here is not to find the most probable candidate from a finite set but rather to *verify* the likelihood that Batenkov's poems and the disputed poems were produced by a single author.
— Finally, we compare the disputed poems not only to Batenkov's established works but also to Iliushin's own poems. The task is, thus, reformulated as a *classification* problem.

4.2.1 Features

A full-scale replication of Shapir's study cannot be undertaken with large corpora because of the limitations of automated text analysis and scansion. We therefore confine our analysis to three levels:
— *Vocabulary* modelled by *lemmata frequencies* (with lemmatisation provided by MyStem 3.1, https://yandex.ru/dev/mystem/);
— *Morphology* modelled indirectly by character 3-grams (excluding punctuation and including blank spaces);
— *Versification* modelled by the rhyme features described in Section 2.2 (rhyme recognition provided by RhymeTagger (Plecháč 2018); IPA transcription provided by Espeak, http://espeak.sourceforge.net/). We do not consider rhythmic features because of the scarcity of lines in any particular metre in the data for either Batenkov or pseudo-Batenkov.

4.2.2 Fine-Tuning

Our first goal is to determine the most efficient feature space. To do this, we train multiple models with the following sets:
(1) frequencies of the *n* most common lemmata (L),
(2) frequencies of the *n* most common character 3-grams (G),
(3) frequencies of the *n* most common lemmata and the *n* most common character 3-grams (LG) and
(4) frequencies of the *n* most common lemmata and the *n* most common character 3-grams enriched with rhyme characteristics (LGR).

This is done for 40 different values of the most common types: $n \in \{50, 100, 150, ..., 2000\}$.

Here we use a corpus of Russian poems whose composition dates to the 1820s. This is partitioned into 200-line samples. Multiple poems can be combined in a single sample, and no poem contributes to more than one sample. This generates:

— 19 samples by Yevgeny Baratynsky,
— 23 samples by Mikhail Lermontov,
— 60 samples by Alexander Pushkin,
— 12 samples by Pyotr Vyazemsky,
— 36 samples by Nikolay Yazykov and
— 11 samples by Vasily Zhukovsky.

We apply the two different classifiers that will be used in subsequent experiments: linear SVM and cosine Delta.

To train the models, we follow the design laid out in Section 3.2. with five randomly selected authors and 10 randomly selected samples. Over 30 iterations, we perform cross-validation for the SVM model and nearest neighbour classification with the Delta approach.

The results can be seen in FIG. 4.4. The performance is similar to those recorded for other languages (Chapter 3): for all of the feature sets, accuracy generally increases to approximately the level of the 1000 most common types. At that point, it stabilises. For both classifiers, the LG combination tends to significantly outperform both L and G on their own. Even greater accuracy is almost always achieved, however, when rhyme features are also taken into account (LGR).

In the next set of experiments, we therefore retain LGR-based models and choose the 1000 most common types as the optimal level.

4.2.3 The One-Class Problem (Authorship Verification)

So far all the tasks we have considered in this book have involved authorship *classification*. In this situation, there is a closed set of candidates $\{A_1, A_2, A_3, ..., A_n\}$ and the goal is to determine which one is most likely the author of the text(s) X. In contrast, authorship *verification* deals with a different scenario. Here it is not possible to determine a closed set that we are sure includes the real author. The goal is instead to decide whether a certain A *is* or *is not* the author of X.

The Batenkov case needs to be treated first and foremost as a verification problem. If there are doubts about the origin of the disputed texts, then we first need to

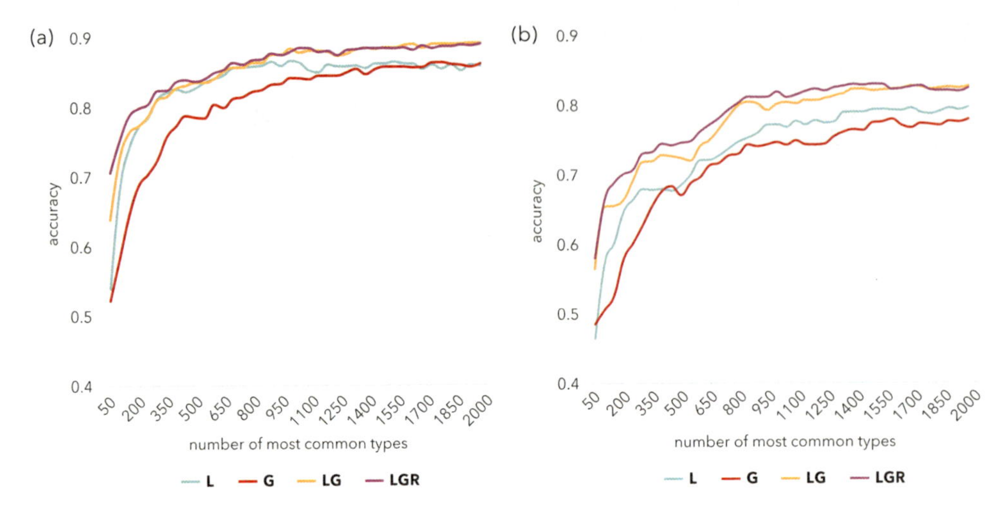

FIG. 4.4: Accuracy of (a) the SVM model and (b) the cosine Delta model with the most common lemmata (L), the most common character 3-grams (G), the L and G combination (LG) and the L and G combination enriched by rhyme features (LGR) across different levels of the most common types.

determine how likely it is that Batenkov himself wrote them regardless of Iliushin's status as a potential author. Here we loosely apply the unmasking technique (Koppel and Schler 2004; Koppel et al. 2007). In its classic version, this technique makes a series of pairwise SVM classifications between same-author and other-author samples. It then iteratively drops the most distinctive features from the learning process. Compared to other verification techniques such as those based on entropy or deep learning (Halvani et al. 2019), unmasking stands out for its clear assumptions and production of interpretable results.

Unmasking assumes that text samples from the same author will share deeper similarities than the samples of two different authors. In the former case, there may still be differences but they will emerge from high-level features such as theme, chronology or genre and not from the underlying style. Moreover, such features will inevitably be exploited by machine classification. That is why the original unmasking method relies on several stages of classification: in each iteration, a certain number of the most distinctive features are dropped and the classification is performed again. Given their underlying similarity, same-author samples should, thus, quickly become indistinguishable from one another while other-author samples retain their differences across many iterations. This is because their "distinctiveness" is distributed over many features and not concentrated in a few high-performing ones.

Since multiple poems can be combined in a single sample and no poem contributes to more than one sample, there is no reason to suppose that any high-level features distinguish the works of a single author. We therefore tweak the classic unmasking process by asking a simple question: Can the known Batenkov poems be distinguished from the disputed poems in a pairwise SVM classification?

To gauge the accuracy of this technique, we also test it on a control group of works published by other Russian poets in the 1840s and 1850s (i.e. the period when the majority of the disputed texts had allegedly been written). Like the Batenkov poems and the disputed poems, these works are divided into 100-line samples. (A 200 line size would generate only three samples from both Batenkov's work and the disputed poems). This produces:

— 13 samples by Mikhail Lermontov,
— 14 samples by Fyodor Tyutchev,
— 18 samples by Pyotr Vyazemsky,
— 15 samples by Nikolay Yazykov,
— six samples by Gavriil Batenkov and
— six samples from the disputed poems.

We then follow the four steps below:

(1) Randomly select 12 samples from each of the four "control" authors.
(2) Randomly split each group of 12 samples in half. These two groups are the A-samples and B-samples.
(3) Use the A-samples and the LGR feature set to train SVM models for each possible pair of "control" authors (i.e. Lermontov vs. Tyutchev, Lermontov vs. Vyazemsky, through to Vyazemsky vs. Yazykov). Perform *leave-one-out* cross-validation of each model.
(4) Train the SVM models with the LGR feature set for each "control" author using his own A-samples and B-samples as separate classes (i.e. Lermontov (A) vs. Lermontov (B), Tyutchev (A) vs. Tyutchev (B), Vyazemsky (A) vs. Vyazemsky (B), Yazykov (A) vs. Yazykov(B)). Perform *leave-one-out* cross-validation of each model.

We repeat this entire process 30 times for each quantity of the most common types: $n \in \{50, 100, 150, \ldots, 1000\}$. A new set of randomly selected samples is used in each iteration. For each n, we therefore obtain $4 \times 30 = 120$ accuracy estimations for samples written by the same author and $\binom{4}{2} \times 30 = 180$ accuracy estimations for samples written by different authors. Finally, for each n, we also cross-validate the Batenkov poems against the disputed poems model.

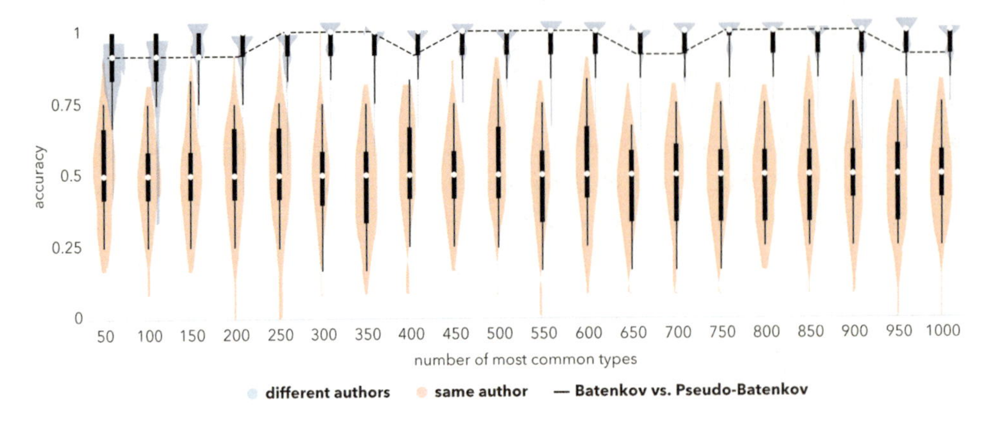

FIG. 4.5: Accuracy of pairwise classifications for different quantities of the most common feature types. Boxplots depict the median, the interquartile range (box) and the 5th-to-95th percentile range (whiskers).

FIG. 4.5 shows the results. The "control" authors behave as might be expected. The median classification accuracy for same-author pairs (A-samples vs. B-samples) hovers around 50%, meaning that on average they are indistinguishable for a classifier. At the same time, accuracy remains high for the pairwise classification of different authors as well. The dashed line in FIG 4.5. represents the classification accuracy for Batenkov poems vs. disputed poems. Without exception, this line follows the general trend for texts from two different sources.

Although these results seem fairly convincing on their own, we wish to go one step further and interpret them in terms of probabilities. As there appears to be no significant divergence among different quantities of the most common words (except perhaps when using the lowest values to classify different authors), we merge all of the values to obtain accuracy estimations for: (1) same-author classifications, (2) different-author classifications and (3) Batenkov poems vs. disputed poems classifications. A Mann-Whitney test[24] shows that the probability of these outcomes if Batenkov *was not* the author of the disputed poems is 0.9265 ($U = 111$, $n_1 = 3600$, $n_2 = 20$). In contrast, if Batenkov *was* the author, the probability is less than 10^{-14} ($U = 60618$, $n_1 = 2400$, $n_2 = 20$).

24 As there are always 12 samples, there are only 12 possible outcomes of cross-validation. The variable in question is, thus, not continuous but discrete. We therefore opt for the non-parametric Mann-Whitney test over the perhaps more expected *t*-test.

4.2.4 The Two-Class Problem (Batenkov vs. Iliushin)

There is, however, a fly in the ointment. As we have observed, Batenkov's poems spanned the 1810s to the 1860s with a significant gap from 1825 to 1846 when he was in solitary confinement (see FIG. 4.6 for a more detailed depiction of this output). The disputed poems date almost entirely from the period after his imprisonment. We therefore cannot rule out a scenario also raised by Shapir: during Batenkov's confinement, there might have been a dramatic change in his writing style which would explain the irregularities in the disputed poems. To address this objection, the disputed poems have to be compared with Batenkov's later poems alone.

Unfortunately, there are not enough data to perform a pairwise SVM experiment with only the poems that Batenkov published after his release. We therefore need to switch to the less data-hungry Delta method. We depend here especially on the cosine variation, which has proven to be the most reliable technique with our "control" authors. The problem is, thus, reframed as a classification task.

To begin, we increase the sample size to 200 lines. This produces the following numbers of samples per author:

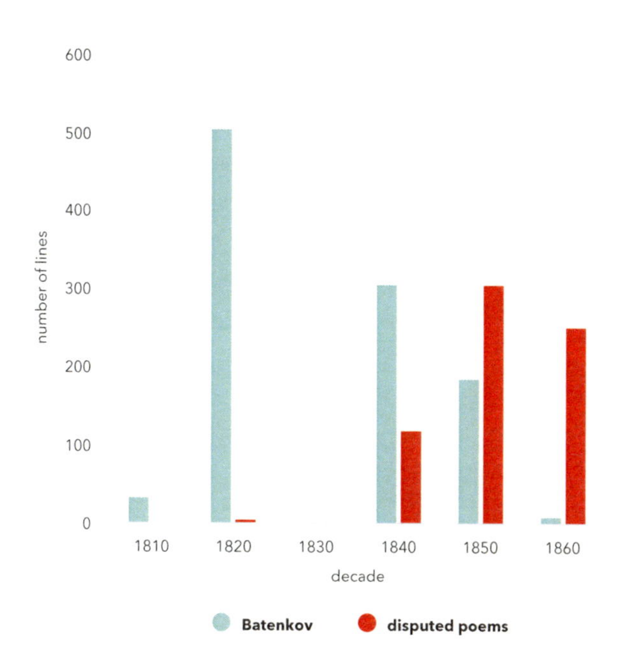

FIG. 4.6: Batenkov's poems and the disputed poems according to their (supposed) composition dates.

— Mikhail Lermontov (8),
— Fyodor Tyutchev (8),
— Pyotr Vyazemsky (12),
— Nikolay Yazykov (8),
— Gavriil Batenkov (2) and
— disputed poems (3).

Over multiple experiments with different feature space settings, the disputed poems remain clustered with Batenkov's poems. This does not say much about the Iliushin hypothesis, however, since the suspected author is not included in the candidate set (if, on the other hand, the disputed poems and Batenkov's poems did not cluster together, this might be interpreted as strong evidence of a forgery).

Although Iliushin never published any poems under his own name, preferring to mask his authorship of non-academic works, several texts have been attributed to him by consensus. These include *Дедушка и девушка* (published as an anonymous poem), *Michele Trivolis — Максим Грек* and *Добрый вампир* (both published under the name Y. F. Sidorin) and *Тайная дочь декабриста Бесстужева...* (the so-called Pseudo-Grigoriev, which was presented as a work by the poet A. Grigoriev, 1822–1864). All of these are long narrative poems from which it is possible to extract a sample comparable to those used in our past experiments.

Now we add the (apparent) Iliushin samples to the corpus and perform another battery of experiments. The quantity of most common types is set to 1000 for both lemmata and character 3-grams. To verify the robustness of these results, we perform 10,000 classifications; in each iteration, 0–1000 types of each feature are dropped from the classification (both the quantity of types and the features themselves are randomly selected). The results are summarised in a confusion matrix (TAB. 4.3).

	Batenkov	**Iliushin**	**Lermontov**	**disputed poems**	**Tyutchev**	**Vyazemsky**	**Yazykov**
Batenkov	**1**			0.06			
Iliushin		**0.99**	0.01	0.21		0.09	
Lermontov			**0.89**		0.03		
disputed poems			0.02	**0.73**			
Tyutchev			0.03		**0.95**	0.01	
Vyazemsky		0.01	0.04		0.01	**0.89**	
Yazykov			0.01		0.01		**1**

TAB. 4.3: Confusion matrix (relative counts). Rows represent the author predicted by the model while columns represent the actual author. Individual cells show the relative number of predictions in each case.

In over 20% of the vector spaces, one sample of the disputed poems appears to be closer to Iliushin's poems than to the other disputed poem samples. This is completely unlike the pattern with the other authors, which showed only minimal variation across the predictions.

Interestingly enough, all of these "misattributions" of the disputed poems to Iliushin concern just two of his samples. These are both poems published under the name Y. F. Sidorin. This, in turn, raises a question: Do these works differ somehow from the other two Iliushin samples?

There are indeed several differences beginning at the level of metre. The Sidorinian poems are written in iambic pentameter, one of the most common metres in Russian poetry in the first half of the 19th century; in contrast, *Дедушка и девушка* is loosely trochaic and "PseudoGrigoriev" is dactylic. Clearly, vocabulary, morphology and rhyme structure can all be profoundly affected by the choice of metre as well.

A closer look at the Sidorinian poems yields even more information. FIG. 4.7 shows the cosine distances across various quantities (50, 100, 150, ..., 2000) of the most common types when the disputed poems are compared with (i) the Sidorinian poems and (ii) Batenkov's own poems published between the 1840s and the 1860s. In all of the

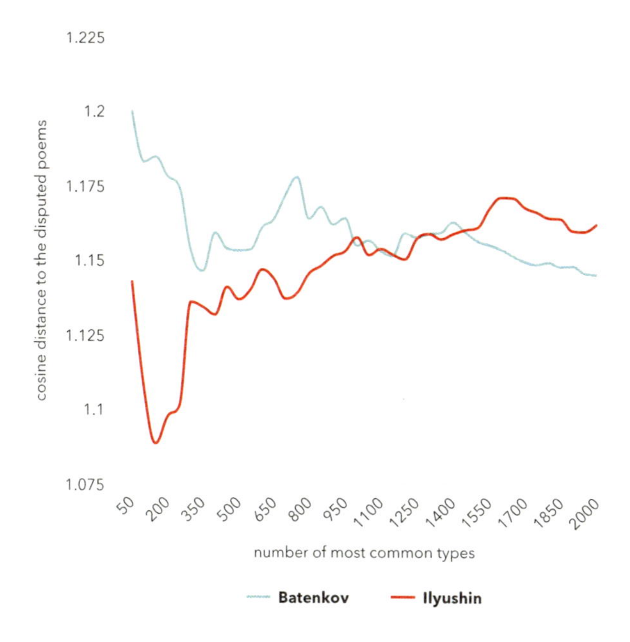

FIG. 4.7: Cosine distances between the disputed poems and (1) the Sidorinian poems (Iliushin) and (2) Batenkov's own poems published between the 1840s and the 1860s for different quantities of the most common types.

vector spaces defined by up to the 1000 most common types, the Sidorinian poems appear to be closer to the disputed poems than Batenkov's own texts are. Then, after a spell in which the distances are more or less even, Batenkov becomes the preferred candidate. This, in fact, seems to be precisely the behaviour we would expect from a forger. Wouldn't such a person imitate an author's obvious idiosyncracies (low-frequency features) but fail to adopt the less obvious ones (high-frequency features like function words and common suffixes)?

4.2.5 Summary

These results do not leave much scope for agreement with Shapir about the essential unverifiability of the disputed poems. As we have seen, when we attempt to treat these texts like original works by Batenkov, they behave radically differently from what we would expect of 19th-century poems written by a single author. Moreover when we try to classify them, they are mistaken for Iliushin's original poetry far more often than they are for the works of their alleged author.

These findings, however, should not be treated as definitive proof of a forgery. After all, stylometry never delivers definitive answers. We are always left with some uncertainty about classification accuracy. The disputed texts may include some unknown original lines later heavily edited or rewritten by the custodians of Batenkov's manuscripts or those who came to study them. And indeed Batenkov may have survived some personality-altering experiences that suddenly rewired his writing habits. Since, however, we have found no evidence to support these possibilities, we would suggest that from now on the null hypothesis should be that "the Batenkov and pseudo-Batenkov texts were not written by the same author".

In practical terms, our results are not surprising since so many scholars and readers remain convinced of Iliushin's forgery despite Shapir's insistence on indeterminate authorship. There are, however, larger theoretical questions at stake: Does language reflect an author's identity? Can a reader recognise the distinctive features of literary style? Are these stylistic features associated with authorship?

Shapir (2000) writes: "Anything conceived by chance, which is unique and unrepeatable, cannot be compared; anything stable and recurring can be abstracted and replicated" (419). The whole history of stylometry reflects an ongoing quest for a means to compare the unique. The methods we rely on seek to access low-level linguistic features that vary greatly among individuals, who usually do not exercise conscious control over them.

Still, stylometry does not give us access to literary forms or any perceived abstract features of a text. How much can we know about Batenkov's literary techniques by observing the distinctive linguistic features of his poetry? Perhaps something from a handful of nouns and verbs, less from pronouns and adverbs and next to nothing from his habit of ending rhymes with a particular sound [x] and his overuse of the character bigrams "ви" and "ен".

Shapir's words speak to the hope of finding the author's identity in linguistic phenomena that can be conceptualised and connected back to literary forms. His work on Batenkov reportedly failed to show this: the authorial signal became fuzzy and the results remained inconclusive. Shapir's uncertainty may find support from recent studies that show that differences in how literary contemporaries use cultural forms and devices ("anything that can be replicated") may be negligible and incomparable to the gigantic gaps between them in the literary market or academic canon (Moretti 2013: 145–147; Porter 2018; Sobchuk 2018: 91–97). Stylistic identity is not, however, bound to any skewed power-law distribution: unlike fame, critical attention and other goods of the symbolic economy, it is distributed equally across the population. That is why stylometry works: everyone who writes is an author.

References

Abney, S. (2007). Semisupervised Learning for Computational Linguistics. Boca Raton, London and New York: CRC.

Al-Falahi, A., Ramdani, M. and Bellafkih, M. (2017). Machine learning for authorship attribution in Arabic poetry. International Journal of Future Computer and Communication, 6(2), 42–46. doi: 10.18178/ijfcc.2017.6.2.486.

Argamon, S. (2008). Interpreting Burrows's Delta: Geometric and probabilistic foundations. Literary and Linguistic Computing, 23(2), 131–147. doi: 10.1093/llc/fqn003.

Baayen, R. H. (2001). Word Frequency Distributions. Dordrecht: Kluwer Academic Publishers. doi: 10.1007/978-94-010-0844-0.

Bobenhausen, K. (2011). The Metricalizer. Automated metrical markup for German poetry. In C. Küper (ed.), Curent Trends in Metrical Analysis. Frankfurt am Main et al.: Peter Lang, 119–131. doi: 10.3726/978-3-653-00980-4.

Bobenhausen, K. and Hammerich, B. (2015). Métrique littéraire, métrique linguistique et métrique algorithmique de l'allemand mises en jeu dans le programme Metricalizer[2]. Langages, 199, 67–87. doi: 10.3917/lang.199.0067.

Boyle, R. (1882). Massinger and *The Two Noble Kinsmen*. New Shakspere Society Transactions 1880–1885, 371–399.

Burrows, J. F. (1989). "An ocean where each kind": Statistical analysis and some major determinants of literary style. Computers and the Humanities, 23(4–5), 309–321. doi: 10.1007/BF02176636.

Burrows, J. F. (2002) "Delta": A measure of stylistic difference and a guide to likely authorship. Literary and Linguistic Computing, 17(3), 267–287. doi: 10.1093/llc/17.3.267.

Burrows, J. F. (2003). Questions of authorship: Attribution and beyond. Computers and the Humanities, 37(1), 5–32. doi: 10.1023/A:1021814530952.

Burrows, J. F. and Hassall, A. J. (1988). Anna Boleyn and the Authenticity of Fielding's Feminine Narrative. Eighteenth-Century Studies, 21(4), 427–453. doi: 10.2307/2738901.

Craig, H. and Kinney, A. F. (2009). Shakespeare, Computers and the Mystery of Authorship. Cambridge: Cambridge University Press. doi: 10.1017/CBO9780511605437.

Čech, R. and Popescu, I.-I. and Altmann, G. (2011). Euphony in Slovak lyric poetry. Glottometrics, 22, 5–16.

Červenka, M. (1998). Máchovo místo ve vývoji českého verše. Česká literatura, 46(5), 485–489.

Červenka, M. and Sgallová, K. (1978). Český verš. In Z. Kopczyńska and L. Pszczołowska (eds.), Słowiańska metryka porównawcza I. Słownik rytmiczny i sposoby jego wykorzystania. Wrocław et al.: Ossolineum, 45–94.

https://doi.org/10.14712/9788024648903.6

De Morgan, A. (1851/1882). To Rev. W. Heald, Aug. 18, 1851 [letter]. In S. E. de Morgan (ed.), Memoir of Augustus de Morgan. London: Longmans, Green, & Co., 214–216.

Diederich, J., Kindermann, J., Leopold, E. and Paass, G. (2003). Authorship attribution with support vector machines. Applied Intelligence, 19(1), 109–123. doi: 10.1023/A:1023824908771.

Dobritsyn, A. (2016). Rhythmic entropy as a measure of rhythmic diversity (The example of Russian iambic tetrameter). Studia Metrica et Poetica, 3(1), 33–52. doi: 10.12697/smp.2016.3.1.02.

Eddy, H. (1887). The characteristic curve of composition. Science, 9(216), 297. doi: 10.1126/science.ns-9.214S.237.

Eder, M. (2011). Style markers in authorship attribution. A cross-language study of the authorial fingerprint. Studies in Polish Linguistics, 6, 99–114.

Eder, M. (2016). Rolling stylometry. Digital Scholarship in the Humanities, 31(3), 457–469. doi: 10.1093/llc/fqv010.

Eisen, M., Riberio, A., Segarra, S. and Egan, G. (2017). Stylometric analysis of early modern period English plays. Digital Scholarship in the Humanities, 33(3), 500–528. doi: 10.1093/llc/fqx059.

Farnham, W. (1916). Colloquial contractions in Beaumont, Fletcher, Massinger and Shakespeare as a test of authorship. Publications of the Modern Language Association of America, 31, 326–358. doi: 10.1632/456960.

Fleay, F. G. (1874a). On the authorship of *The Taming of the Shrew*. Transactions of the New Shakspere Society, 1, 85–129.

Fleay, F. G. (1874b). On the authorship of *Timon of Athens*. Transactions of the New Shakspere Society, 1, 130–194.

Fleay, F. G. (1874c). A fresh confirmation of Mr. Spedding's division and date of the play of *Henry VIII*. Transactions of the New Shakspere Society, 1, appendix 23.

Fleay, F. G. (1874d). Mr. Hickson's division of *The Two Noble Kinsmen*, confirmed by Metrical Tests. Transactions of the New Shakspere Society, 1, appendix 61–64.

Forstall, C. W., Jacobson, S. L. and Scheirer, W. J. (2011). Evidence of intertextuality: investigating Paul the Deacon's *Angustae Vitae*. Literary and Linguistic Computing, 26(3), 285–296. doi: 10.1093/llc/fqr029.

Forstall, C. W. and Scheirer, W. J. (2010). A statistical stylistic study of Latin elegiac couplets. 2010 Chicago Colloquium on Digital Humanities and Computer Science Abstracts, Evanston: Northwestern University, 21–22. 11.

Fucks, W. (1952). On mathematical analysis of style. Biometrika, 39(1–2): 122–129. doi: 10.1093/biomet/39.1-2.122.

Furnivall, F. J. (1874a). The founder's prospectus of the New Shakspere Society. Transactions of the New Shakspere Society, 1, appendix 6–7.

Furnivall, F. J. (1874b). Another fresh confirmation of Mr. Spedding's division and date of the play of *Henry VIII*. Transactions of the New Shakspere Society, 1, appendix 24.

Furnivall, F. J. (1874c). Mr. Hickson's division of *The Two Noble Kinsmen*, confirmed by the the stopt-line test. Transactions of the New Shakspere Society, 1, appendix 64–65.

Gasparov, M. and Tarlinskaja, M. (2008). The Linguistics of Verse. The Slavic and East European Journal, 52(2), 198–207.

Giesbrecht, E. and Evert, S. (2009). Is Part-of-Speech Tagging a Solved Task? An Evaluation of POS Taggers for the German Web as Corpus. In I. Alegria, I. Leturia and S. Sharoff (eds.), Proceedings of the 5th Web as Corpus Workshop (WAC5). San Sebastian.

Göhring, A. (2009). Spanish Expansion of a Parallel Treebank. Master's thesis. Universität Zürich.
Grieve, J. (2005). Quantitative authorship attribution: A history and an evaluation of techniques. Master's thesis. Simon Fraser University.
Grzybek, P. (2014). The emergence of stylometry: prolegomena to the history of term and concept. In: Kroó, Katalin; Torop, Peeter (eds.), Text within Text — Culture within Culture. Budapest, Tartu: L'Harmattan, 58–75.
Hajič, J. (2004). Disambiguation of Rich Inflection (Computational Morphology of Czech). Prague: Karolinum.
Halvani, O., Winter, C. and Graner, L. (2019). Assessing the Applicability of Authorship Verification Methods. In Proceedings of the 14th International Conference on Availability, Reliability and Security (ARES '19). New York: Association for Computing Machinery, 1–10. doi: 10.1145/3339252.3340508.
Hart, A. (1934). Shakespeare and the vocabulary of The Two Noble Kinsmen. The Review of English Studies, 10(39), 274–287.
Herdan, G. (1956). Chaucer's authorship of the Equatorie of the Planetis: The use of romance vocabulary as evidence. Language, 32(2), 254–259.
Hickson, S. (1847). The shares of Shakespeare and Fletcher in *The Two Noble Kinsmen*. The Westminster and Foreign Quarterly Review, 47, 59–48
Holmes, D. I. (1998). The evolution of stylometry in humanities scholarship. Literary and Linguistic Computing, 13(3), 111–117. doi: 10.1093/llc/13.3.111.
Hoover, D. L. (2003). Another perspective on vocabulary richness. Computers and the Humanities, 37(2), 151–178. doi: 10.1023/A:1022673822140.
Hoover, D. L. (2004a). Testing Burrows's Delta. Literary and Linguistic Computing, 19(4), 453–475. doi: 10.1093/llc/19.4.453.
Hoover, D. L. (2004b). Delta Prime? Literary and Linguistic Computing, 19(4), 477–495. doi: 10.1093/llc/19.4.477.
Horsmann, T., Erbs, N. and Zesch, T. (2015). Fast or accurate? A comparative evaluation of PoS tagging models. In Proceedings of the International Conference of the German Society for Computational Linguistics and Language Technology (GSCL-2015).
Horton, T. B. (1987). The Effectiveness of the Stylometry of Function Words in Discriminating between Shakespeare and Fletcher. Dissertation. Edinburgh: University of Edinburgh.
Hoy, C. (1962). The Shares of Fletcher and his collaborators in the Beaumont and Fletcher Canon VII. Studies in Bibliography, 15, 71–90.
Iliushin, A. A. (1978). Poeziia dekabrista Gavriila Stepanovitcha Batenkova. Moscow: Izdatelstvo MGU.
Iliushin, E. A. (ed.). (2020). Izbrannyie stikhotvornie proizviedienia. Moscow: Common Place.
Ingram, J. K. (1874). On the "weak endings" of Shakspere, with some account of the history of the verse tests in general. Transactions of the New Shakspere Society, 1, 442–456.
Jakobson, R. (1938/1995). K popisu Máchova verše. In idem: Poetická funkce. Jinočany: H & H, 427–476,
Jannidis, F., Pielström, S., Schöch, C. and Vitt, T. (2015). Improving Burrows' Delta. An empirical evaluation of text distance measures. Digital Humanities Conference 2015, Sydney.
Jirát, V. (1931–1932). Hudebnost Máchova rýmu. Časopis pro moderní filologii 18(1–2), 24–34 & 147–157.

Juola, P. (2006). Authorship attribution. Foundations and Trends in Information Retrieval, 1(3), 233–334. doi: 10.1561/1500000005.
Kestemont, M. and Haverals, W. (2018). Metrical analyses of medieval Dutch poetry for the purpose of genre and authorship analysis [conference paper]. Plotting Poetry II: Bringing Deep Learning to Computational Poetry Analysis. Berlin: Freie Universität Berlin, 12.–14. 9. 2018.
Koppel, M. and Schler, J. (2004). Authorship verification as a one-class classification problem. Proceedings of the 21st International Conference on Machine Learning. New York: ACM, 62–68. doi: 10.1145/1015330.1015448.
Koppel, M., Schler, J. and Argamon, S. (2009). Computational methods in authorship attribution. Journal of the Association for Information Science and Technology, 60(1), 9–26. doi: 10.1002/asi.20961.
Koppel, M., Schler, J. and Bonchek-Dokow, E. (2007) Measuring Differentiability: Unmasking Pseudonymous Authors. Journal of Machine Learning Research, 8, 1261–1276.
Larsen, W. A., Rencher, A. C. and Layton, T. (1980). Who wrote the *Book of Mormon*? An analysis of wordprints. BYU Studies Quarterly, 20(3), 225–251.
Ledger, G. and Merriam, T. (1994). Shakespeare, Fletcher, and *The Two Noble Kinsmen*. Literary and Linguistic Computing, 9(3), 235–248. doi: 10.1093/llc/9.3.235.
Lotman, J. M. and Lotman, M. (1986). Vokrug desjatoj glavy "Evgenija Onegina". In N. N. Petrunina (ed.), Pushkin: Issledovanija i materialy XII. Moscow/Leningrad: Nauka, 124–151.
Malone, Edmond. (1787/1803). A dissertation on parts one, two and three of *Henry the Sixth* tending to show that those plays were not written originally by Shakespeare. In Plays of William Shakespeare 14. London, 219–263.
Mascol, C. (1888a). Curves of pauline and pseudo-pauline style I. Unitarian Review, 30, 452–460.
Mascol, C. (1888b). Curves of Pauline and Pseudo-Pauline style II. Unitarian Review, 30, 539–546.
Matthews, R. and Merriam, T. (1993). Neural computation in stylometry I; An application to the works of Shakespeare and Fletcher. Literary and Linguistic Computing, 8(4), 203–209. doi: 10.1093/llc/8.4.203.
Mendenhall, T. C. (1887). The characteristic curves of composition. Science, 9(214), 237–249.
Mendenhall, T. C. (1901). A mechanical solution to a literary problem. Popular Science Monthly, 9, 97–110.
Mikros, G. K. and Perifanos, K. A. (2013). Authorship attribution in Greek tweets using author's multilevel *n*-gram profile. In Papers from the 2013 AAAI Spring Symposium. "Analyzing Microtext", 25–27 March 2013. Palo Alto: AAAI Press, 17–23.
Mittmann, A., Pergher, P. H. and dos Santos, A. L. 2019. What rhythmic signature says about poetic corpora. In P. Plecháč, B. Scherr, T. Skulacheva, H. Bermúdez-Sabel and R. Kolár (eds.), Quantitative Approaches to Versification. Prague: ICL, 153–172.
Moretti, F. (2013). Distant Reading. NY: Verso.
Mosteller, F. and Wallace D. L. (1964). Inference and Disputed Authorship. Reading: Addison-Wesley.
Nagy, B. (2021). Metre as a stylometric feature in Latin hexameter poetry. Digital Scholarship in the Humanities [advance articles]. doi: 10.1093/llc/fqaa043.
Navarro-Colorado, B. (2015). A computational linguistic approach to Spanish Golden Age sonnets: metrical and semantic aspects. Computational Linguistics for Literature NAACL 2015, Denver (Co). doi: 10.3115/v1/W15-0712.

Navarro-Colorado, B. (2017). A metrical scansion system for fixed-metre Spanish poetry. Digital Scholarship in the Humanities, 33(1), 112–127. doi: 10.1093/llc/fqx009.

Navarro-Colorado, B., Ribes-Lafoz, M. and Sánchez, N. (2016). Metrical annotation of a large corpus of Spanish sonnets. Representation, scansion and evaluation. Proceedings of the Tenth International Conference on Language Resources and Evaluation (LREC 2016). Portorož.

Oliphant, E. H. C. (1891). The Works of Beaumont and Fletcher. Englische Studien 15, 321–360.

Oras, A. (1953). "Extra monosyllables" in *Henry VIII* and the problem of authorship. Journal of English and Germanic Philology, 52, 198–213.

Platt, J. (1999). Probabilistic outputs for support vector machines and comparisons to regularized likelihood methods. Advances in Large Margin Classifiers, 10(3), 61–74.

Plecháč, P. (2016). Czech verse processing system KVĚTA: Phonetic and metrical components. Glottotheory, 7, 159–174. doi: 10.1515/glot-2016-0013.

Plecháč, P. (2018). A collocation-driven method of discovering rhymes (in Czech, English, and French poetry). In M. Fidler and V. Cvrček (eds.), Taming the Corpus. From Inflection and Lexis to Interpretation. Cham: Springer, 79–95. doi: 10.1007/978-3-319-98017-1_5.

Plecháč, P. (2020). Relative contributions of Shakespeare and Fletcher in *Henry VIII*: An analysis based on most frequent words and most frequent rhythmic patterns. Digital Scholarship in the Humanities [advance articles]. doi: 10.1093/llc/fqaa032.

Plecháč, P. and Birnbaum, D. (2019). Assessing the reliability of stress as a feature of authorship attribution in syllabic and accentual syllabic verse. In P. Plecháč, B. P. Scherr, T. Skulacheva, H. Bermúdez-Sabel, R. Kolár (eds.), Quantitative Approaches to Versification. Prague: ICL CAS, 201–210.

Plecháč, P., Bobenhausen, K. and Hammerich, B. (2018). Versification and authorship attribution. Pilot study on Czech, German, Spanish, and English Poetry. Studia Metrica et Poetica, 5(2), 29–54. doi: 10.12697/smp.2018.5.2.02.

Plecháč, P., Kolár, R. (2015). The Corpus of Czech Verse. Studia Metrica et Poetica, 2(1), 107–118. doi: 10.12697/smp.2015.2.1.05.

Porter, J. D. (2018). Popularity/Prestige. Pamphlets of Stanford Literary Lab, 17.

Rybicki, J. and Eder, M. (2011). Deeper Delta across genres and languages: Do we really need the most frequent words? Literary and Linguistic Computing, 26(3), 315–321. doi: 10.1093/llc/fqr031.

Savoy, J. (2020). Advanced models for stylometric application. In: Machine Learning Methods for Stylometry. Authorship Attribution and Author Profiling. Cham: Springer, 153–187. doi: 10.1007/978-3-030-53360-1_7.

Schmid, H. (1994). Probabilistic part-of-speech tagging using decision trees. In Proceedings of International Conference on New Methods in Language Processing. Manchester.

Segarra, S., Eisen, M. and Riberio, A. (2013). Authorship attribution using function words adjacency networks. In International Conference on Acoustics, Speech and Signal Processing (ICASSP). IEEE, 5563–5567. doi: 10.1109/ICASSP.2013.6638728.

Shapir, M. I. (1997). Fenomen Batenkova i problema mistifikatsii (lingvistikhovedcheskij aspekt 1–2). Philologica, 4, 85–144.

Shapir, M. I. (1998). Fenomen Batenkova i problema mistifikatsii (lingvistikhovedcheskij aspekt 3–4). Philologica, 5, 49–132.

Shapir, M. I. (2000). Fenomen Batenkova i problema mistifikatsii. In M. I. Shapir. Universum versus: Iazyk — stikh — smysl v russkoi poezii XVIII-XIX vekov, 1. Moscow: Yazyki russkoi kultury, 335–443.

Sherman, L. A. (1888). Some observations upon sentence-length in English prose. The University of Nebraska Studies, 1(4), 337–366.

Skoumalová, H. (2011). Porovnání úspěšnosti tagování korpusu. In V. Petkevič and A. Rosen (eds.), Korpusová lingvistika Praha 2011/3. Gramatika a značkování korpusů. Prague: Nakladatelství Lidové Noviny, 199–207.

Smith, P. W. H. and Aldridge, W. (2011). Improving authorship attribution: Optimizing Burrows' Delta method. Journal of Quantitative Linguistics, 18(1), 63–88. doi: 10.1080/09296174.2011.533591.

Sobchuk O. (2018). Charting Artistic Evolution: An Essay in Theory. Dissertation. Tartu: University of Tartu Press, 2018.

Spalding, W. (1833). A Letter on Shakespeare's Authorship of *The Two Noble Kinsmen*. Edinburgh: A. & C. Black.

Spedding, J. (1850). Who wrote Shakespeare's *Henry VIII*? The Gentlemen's Magazine, 115–123.

Spoustová, D., Hajič, J., Votrubec, J., Krbec, P. and Květoň, P. (2007). The best of two worlds: Cooperation of statistical and rule-based taggers for Czech. Proceedings of the Workshop on Balto-Slavonic Natural Language Processing. ACL, 67–74.

Tabata, T. (2012). Approaching Dickens' style through random forests. Digital Humanities 2012: Conference Abstracts. Hamburg: Universität Hamburg, 388–391.

Tarlinskaja, M. (1987). Shakespeare's Verse: Iambic Pentameter and the Poet's Idiosyncrasies. New York: Peter Lang.

Tarlinskaja, M. (2014). Shakespeare and the Versification of English Drama, 1561–1642. Farnham et al.: Ashgate.

Thorndike, A. H. (1901). The Influence of Beaumont and Fletcher on Shakespeare. Worcester: Oliver B. Wood.

Tomashevsky, B. V. (1923/2008). Pjatistopnyj jamb Pushkina. In Izbrannye raboty o stikhe. Moscow & Sankt Peterburg: Akademija, 140–242.

Vickers, B. (2004). Shakespeare, Co-Author. A Historical Study of Five Collaborative Plays. Oxford: Oxford University Press. doi: 10.1093/acprof:oso/9780199269167.001.0001.

Weber, H. (1812). Observations on the participation of Shakespeare in *The Two Noble Kinsmen*. In H. Weber (ed.), The Works of Beaumont and Fletcher in Fourteen Volumes 13. Edinburgh: J. Ballantyne & Co., 151–169.

Williams, C. B. (1975). Mendenhall's studies of word-length distribution in the works of Shakespeare and Bacon. Biometrika, 62(1), 207–212. doi: 10.1093/biomet/62.1.207.

Yule, G. U. (1939). On sentence-length as a statistical characteristic of style in prose, with application to two cases of disputed authorship. Biometrika, 30, 363–390.

Yule, G. U. (1944). The Statistical Study of Literary Vocabulary. Cambridge: Cambridge University Press.

Zhao, Y. and Zobel, J. (2005). Effective and scalable authorship attribution using function words. In G. G. Lee et al. (eds.), Information Retrieval Technology. AIRS 2005. Lecture Notes in Computer Science. Berlin and Heidelberg: Springer, 174–189. doi: 10.1007/11562382_14.

Zipf, G. K. (1932). Selected Studies on the Principle of Relative Frequency in Language. Cambridge, MA: Harvard Uniersity Press.